What p

Haunted: Horror of Haverfordwest

G L Davies is an author who leads the reader through a gripping account of his own personal haunting which I found to be very interesting. Through his experience, he has gained an unusual insight into what can happen to a normal person when they happen across The Paranormal. This chilling read will certainly start to worry the reader and will certainly have them looking behind them at some stage. This is a must read for those looking for explanations. As Demonologist on the TV show Most Haunted, I understand what the author went through and this book should not only make people more aware of what to them was previously unknown but make them think twice about meddling with it.
Fred Batt

This is a Terrifying read, a book that will haunt you long after you have read it. Its builds masterfully, drawing you closer and closer and then the terror hits you. This is a modern paranormal masterpiece, complete with the original A most haunted house and a must read section on explanations, this is possibly the most important paranormal account of the 21st Century. This is a haunting people will be talking about in a hundred years time and all the while they will say, I hope it didn't happen in our house. G L Davies is finally back and he has grown as a writer and investigator, this is shocking and chilling brilliance.
K-Town, *Mysterious Radio*

GL Davies takes us into the real life terror of a malevolent haunting in the pages of Haunted: Horror of Haverfordwest. If you have the intestinal fortitude to venture forward, your bravery will be rewarded with a great, if frightening read. I'd say go for it and pick up your copy today!
Jim Harold, host of the *Paranormal Podcast* and *Jim Harold's Campfire*

A paralogian to the paranormal is like a theologian to theology. A paralogian should have a good understanding of paranormal history, theory, & application. It is clearly evident that G L Davies not only has a real solid understanding of the different kinds of paranormal activity & phenomena people may experience, but he also understands the impact in which that said phenomena can have on an individual's psychological well being as well as the parasociological implications for the surrounding family unit. G L Davies is a true paralogian through & through. Haunted: Horror of Haverfordwest is a testament to that statement & a real pleasure to digest.
Kevin Malek, Paranormal Historian and Ufologist

The courage it took to tell a story of the supernatural that drove one to the depths of depression is to be admired. G L Davies accounts are raw, real and riveting.
Jeremy Scott, *Into the Parabnormal Radio*

G L Davies once again takes readers on a terrifying journey into madness and the unknown that will grip believers tightly and shake sceptics to their very core.
Ashley Shannon, *Schlock Tactics Podcast*

If you are a paranormal investigator and have not read this book then you are not a real Paranormal Investigator. Raw, real, detailed, gritty and utterly frightening […] this is the UK's most detailed and prolific modern haunting investigating over twenty years' worth of evidence. There are incidents and events that linger long after reading, things difficult to make sense of, disturbing things that will leave you with you one thought: *I hope this never happens to me*! The best paranormal book out there. Read it, just not before bed.
Nikki Davies, Lead Investigator – *Devon Ghost Adventures*

Haunted:
Horror of
Haverfordwest

Haunted: Horror of Haverfordwest

GL Davies

Winchester, UK
Washington, USA

First published by Sixth Books, 2018
Sixth Books is an imprint of John Hunt Publishing Ltd., No. 3 East St., Alresford,
Hampshire SO24 9EE, UK
office1@jhpbooks.net
www.johnhuntpublishing.com
www.6th-books.com

For distributor details and how to order please visit the 'Ordering' section on our website.

ISBN: 978 1 78535 843 2
978 1 78535 844 9 (ebook)
Library of Congress Control Number: 2017952294

A CIP catalogue record for this book is available from the British Library.

Design: Stuart Davies

UK: Printed and bound by CPI Group (UK) Ltd, Croydon, CR0 4YY
US: Printed and bound by Thomson-Shore, 7300 West Joy Road, Dexter, MI 48130

Contents

Introduction

Fear is pain arising from the anticipation of Evil.
Aristotle

A house should always be a home, an abode of familiarity, a place of refuge. A space one can retreat to, to cultivate hopes and dreams; a place to forge a loving environment. Within its shelter we nurture and birth memory and happiness. A house is where we face the hardships of life, guarded in the confines of our own fabricated setting, personalised with the artefacts of good people and good times. Home is not so much the place but more the feeling. It is our sanctuary.

As adults, we still refer to our parents' home as our home, an ownership not on the property itself but on the feeling of safety and invulnerability. Times of deep worry or doubt dissolve into the steam of a hot cup of tea and familiar parental reassurance, for most at least.

Occasionally that home will betray us. More often than not it is the people we place our love and trust in that destroys this sanctuary. Abuse, dependency, violence, infidelity, parental complacency and neglect are all hammers to the bricks of our psychological bond to what should have been a home.

Though darker still and hidden in the blackness of our nightmares dwells an inexplicable and absolute force. It is a brutal and undefinable element that interferes in our world with no recognisable agenda other than to tear apart the fabric of what makes us human.

It spreads like a mould, cold and rotten, seeping into our thoughts, consuming the joy, decaying the hopes, slaughtering without heed our essence, like lambs at an abattoir. We are left a shell, a decomposing putrid vessel of what should have been a beacon of light, a person that can dream, believe, create and love.

It thrives on our misery; it drinks our negativity and expands in our suffering.

What is this thing so destructive and malevolent?

Some call it demons. Others name it ghosts or evil spirits, while some believe dimensional beings cross through the veil of our known physics to feed on our desolation. It is faceless and nameless in regard to human comprehension. It is something altogether inhuman; it is evil in its nature but evil is again a human concept. To comprehend its motives would be as easy as understanding the nature of the universe. There is only so much the mind can fathom before the elasticity of comprehension snaps and the mind begins to regress. We have to ask, is our melancholic maladies caused by such a thing or could one argue it is the reverse?

In life, some of us live happily, oblivious to the torments that lurk deep within the walls of a home; accounts of ghosts and the paranormal merely stories and imaginations for the weak of mind but active of inventiveness. Yet so many of us feel that momentary panic as we cross the landing in the dark or as we are jolted from a deep sleep by something unseen. Our minds can be haunted by film, TV programs and literature hours and even days after absorbing concepts of such horror, even though we know we are just being preposterous because such things do not and cannot exist. Or do they?

Our minds from birth are shaped by notions of religious miracles and more than human biblical exploits, of Father Christmas and the Easter Bunny. We are surrounded in a world of myth and legend. Magical boys and faraway lands dominate the box office while over fifty per cent of the planet believe in and actively communicate to an invisible omnipresent entity that created all we know. Our lives are foreshadowed by concepts of Heaven and Hell, Good and Evil, life after death, reincarnation, saints and miracles, singular Gods and animal deities, the Holy Spirit, alien life, multiverses, parallel dimensions, and on and on. The mysteries of our lives unfold unconditionally before us yet unanswerable, and still we are told that some things are not acceptable to believe in.

The house in Haverfordwest lingered in my psyche, resistant to any form of catharsis. It dwelt there for nearly a decade before I took action in an attempt to cleanse my brooding and dark thoughts of the experiences that took place there. Day after day my thoughts would dwell on the house, a house unlike any I had lived in before nor would I wish to again.

In 2013, I suffered a nervous breakdown; I had been dependent on alcohol for over a decade since I had lived at the house and found myself staring into the abyss of despair. One small foot away from actions that would have been an absolute end, an escape to the depression and darkness. I pushed everyone I ever loved away and found no joy in life. There was no tomorrow. My dreams were consumed by the house, beckoning with arms of bramble-like vines, windows blackened and cracked, the front door missing, boasting an infinite hole of gloom. I was utterly lost to the light, to what made me who I was. It was time to find closure not in the house – the power in the house was invincible – but on my life.

Some would argue that the house was merely a manifestation of my depression; that it merely represented my bleakness, and that I needed to visualise my fears into something tangible. But I knew that the events of *A most haunted house* were more than just perception; they were a digestion of the events that happened there. Something very real had happened there and it had hollowed out my soul and feasted on my want for life.

On 7th January 2013, the night I decided would be my last, after the consumption of two bottles of rum and several bottles of wine, I did something absolutely baffling and deranged to those that have not been trapped in the quicksand of depression. Rationalists will snigger, but I tried to telephone my dead grandmother.

My gran had died in September 2009, several years before, and she had left a hole in my life that quickly eclipsed any brightness that was left. Her unconditional love had been the counterweight to life's woes, to my failures, to the grasp the house had upon me. I had loved her so much. I thought that by ringing her maybe she would somehow be there, give me a sign that there were better things waiting for me once I had, in my mind, relinquished this vehicle we call a body. Maybe there would be peace waiting for me on the other side. I cannot remember anything more of that night other than my instinct to reach out to her.

Society has a view that to take one's life is the uttermost selfish act that one can perform. However, when you are at that stage, you are stripped of everything that makes you you. Gone are base human qualities such as fear, anger, love. There is no ego or sadness, and all you are left with are two simple options: Do I simply cease to exist? Or do I cease to exist and explore the possibility of a better life after death?

I woke up the next day confusingly free from the effects of such damaging alcohol consumption – amongst the other things unprescribed – with the purpose of neutralising my melancholy. The winter sun shone brightly into the room, and I lay there for a moment and realised there was indeed a flicker of hope inside; that a flame still burnt that wanted so much from this life. That day I attained a desire to smile, to strive, to achieve, to love again. I wanted to live. I, to this day, have no idea what had really happened during that night.

I took the action, the support, I so dearly needed. Friends rallied around and got me help. I changed and removed many damaging aspects of my life, sought professional counsel and re-established myself at the bottom of the ladder and began to climb again, rung by rung. I began to appreciate and feel value in almost everything. I took accountability for my actions and explored the triggers that had taken me down a very dark and dangerous path.

I finally defeated my dependency to alcohol on 23rd March 2013, and have been sober ever since. I took control of my life, reinvented my career and used every day as an opportunity to succeed and accomplish. Every day is a day of warmth and of sunshine; and overcoming my own personal tribulations has allowed me to support and mentor others with dependency issues. I have been blessed with the gift of being able to help others that have stood at the edge of the abyss and to show them that there is hope, that we can turn around and face the sun again. I felt I had not had a nervous and mental breakdown, but a spiritual awakening.

What of the house? Had my experiences there been real? I was asked to confront the issues by the wonderful professionals charged with my healing process, to try and understand what had happened there. Had the events there, the loss and grief, the hurt and pain, manifested the haunting into something that I perceived to be real? I began to write.

The more I wrote the more the events became more real, but gone was my fear, and a duty emerged, a duty to unveil this nefarious force. If I could understand its effect then maybe I could help others or at the very least help heal my own psychological wounds. In October 2013 I finished, while sat at Carmarthen train station, the first draft of what would become *A most haunted house*.

My dear friend Ash had been keen to understand what had happened at the house and asked to read it. I was dubious at first that such a private experience be shared. However, I trusted her and sent her a copy. The next day her partner Ste asked, what had I done to her? Ash has been too scared to go to the loo in the night!

Other friends started to read it and encouraged me to publish it; they said sharing it would help others experiencing the same thing. They loved the mystery of whether it was a haunting or a psychological reaction to the breakdown of the relationship at the house that made the house seem haunted. They said it was troubling and chilling, and very different to what other writers of the genre offered. They said it read as an authentic retelling, a real testimony of very real events affecting real people. There was an emotional attachment to the people involved. They believed it could help others but at the same time they believed it would terrify people too!

I lacked the confidence to publish it as my own personal account. I was deeply concerned that the other people who were part of my life at the time would take great offence if they were linked to a paranormal testimonial, so I fictionalised the names, changed dates and attempted to hide the clues that could cause much bother for the other people involved. I changed my name to John in the testimony. I hid my dependency, depression and failings under the guise of a faceless man. Only I and those very close to me knew it was me, though others guessed in time. The account is 90% accurate in its telling, I just had to change the details of the people. I also had no real idea how some of the others were dealing with their experiences. They had closed ranks and shut me out. It had been something I had faced alone for over ten years.

By merely writing it and sharing it, I felt a huge weight lift from me as I dropped those immense bags of rocks of shame and guilt from having wasted so much of my life in a depressed state; and I decided to self-publish on eReader. I suffer from dyslexia, which is a common learning difficulty that can cause problems with reading, writing and spelling. Intelligence is not affected by this learning disability and it's estimated that up to 1 in every 10 people in the UK (to say nothing of the world) have some degree of dyslexia. Another wonderful side effect from my experience was that I could support and encourage young adults who also were dyslexic to write and explore creative avenues. Unlike many self-publishers I had no illusions of grandeur that my book would be read by anyone other than close friends so I did not hire the services of a proofreader or an editor [*GV Thomas would go on and edit* A most haunted house *later in 2014.*] and that was very much evident in the first issue. I made a cover [*That is me in a wig on the cover of the original for fans of the book.*] and uploaded the Word document and left it at that.

On 1st January 2014, nearly a year after my spiritual awakening and three months after self-publishing, I was notified that my little account was number 1 in several e-reading categories in four countries, and had been read by hundreds of people. I had no clue. I was contacted by publishers offering me deals if I would spice up the action and add more supernatural horror to the account, but I never intended for a sensationalised version of events. *A most haunted house* was a personal catharsis for me, a reminder of the true power of unseen forces at work and the effects on people. How fragile we are psychologically and just as importantly how we can endure as humans and overcome the darkness. *A most haunted house* was my attempt to rationalise whether a prolific haunting in a house in Haverfordwest, West Wales was the cause of the disablement of blissful beginnings or whether the haunting was a manifestation of the breakdown of what should have been an enchanted time in life.

In August of 2015 I was approached by a friendly and empathic journalist named Jean Jollands who had read *A most haunted house* and reached out to me to find out more about the occupants of possibly the most prolific haunting in Haverfordwest (or even in *Wales* as some had suggested) for a magazine called *Take a Break: Fate and Fortune*. I felt the time was right to acknowledge that I had in fact been John and that the account was mine. By this time, I had the blessing of those involved and I felt confident that I was strong enough of mind and emotion to admit my part in the testimony. There was of course criticism from some within the paranormal community for my admission, saying it had been deceitful to hide my identity. In their defence, they did not know the full extent of my breakdown and of my dependency. They did not fully understand that from the safety of my anonymity I was able to grow in confidence and build a new life. I was blessed, however, to have so much love and support from people I knew, from those within the paranormal community and from complete strangers that could relate to my issues, and the strength I found to overcome. That support was incredible and far outweighs any negatives my journey has taken me on. It humbles me to this day.

Nearly four years on, *A most haunted house* has taken on a little life of its own. It has been featured on radio shows and podcasts across the globe, featured in newspapers and magazines, has interest from film and TV production companies and been read by over 50,000 people! The Paranormal Chronicles, which is a project created at the same time to help give me drive, focus and to help me understand the events, has become a global community with over half a million visitors to my blog site. It is an astonishing and humbling social media presence which has offered me the opportunity to create a YouTube channel, The Paranormal Chronicles Network, where myself and like-minded individuals can present and ponder the nature of the paranormal. I have been blessed to have met so many extraordinary and dedicated people who work towards looking for answers to the mysteries that haunt our existence.

A dark and almost soul-destroying episode of my life has blossomed and grown to become a wonderful time, where I can share my past without fear of ridicule or shame with people from all over the world, and we can all offer each other support, not just on matters of the supernatural but on depression, mental health and dependency.

Do I believe that there is a connection between depression and the paranormal? I do. To what degree I do not know but I continue to explore that idea every day of my life.

But again, what of the house?

The more people the book reached the more I felt like I was

defeating the entity that resided there. I was experiencing more positive effects from the book than the negative which had affected me in the past. I was surrounded by people who helped me understand: I was part of something strong. I was part of a network of great people, and together, united, we would not be broken.

Then I received the email.

In September 2015, a few weeks after the *Take a Break: Fate and Fortune* article had been published I received an email from a lady asking many questions about the house.

I began to worry as I had worked very hard to conceal the location of the house. It had been a daily occurrence, nay, a scourge of people asking where the house was. It became a guessing game. Fabricators assuredly told people through social media where the location was and they were wrong. No one guessed, until…

The email asked a great many details about the location of the house. The woman identified first the area and then the street. I was alarmed as this could cause potential issues for the owners of the house, who chose to leave the house unoccupied due to the ongoing situation that troubled many tenants with its paranormal abuse, and planned to sell it.

I felt that ignoring the woman would be discourteous so answered that the house had to remain unidentified due to the circumstances surrounding the current owners. Then she identified not just the street but the actual house, and began to tell me of an experience she and her husband had encountered while living there in 1989. They too had been victims to the intensity of the haunting; they too had been victims to a darkness that prowled the abode. I was obviously dubious but the more we communicated the more it became real. She knew the layout of the house and she knew of things that had not been published in *A most haunted house* as they were surreal aspects of the haunting that were difficult to articulate. Her account was thirteen years before those incidents in *A most haunted house* and shed new and detailed information on the haunting.

I was conflicted between the jubilation that validation brings yet worried that this was something very real and not just a personal psychological infirmity. Could this couple prove that the house was subject to a paranormal transgression? My theories on the events that affected the home were centred on a new mobile communications transmitter based on TETRA Cold War psychological technology, and these soon started to dissolve.

Not only was their account detailed but they experienced a more intense version of what I had for the short time I lived in the house. I do not think I would be here writing this now had I experienced what they had. I honestly believe that the events which happened between 1989 and 1991 to them would have broken me in all perceivable manners. Their testimony coupled with my experiences helped me understand that the paranormal perception like most things in life is based on the individual. My investigation had shown me that some people are more receptive and therefore their experience more detailed, while others experience little to nothing. Paranormal perception can almost be likened to hearing as everyone can hear different frequencies. Some can never hear certain frequencies whilst others are attuned to most.

The couple were willing to share their account but asked for anonymity. They are both in their mid-fifties and still live in Pembrokeshire as do their family, and like many, they feel that they will be open to ridicule and concentrated negativity. We must remember that this is a very challenging subject to many, and certain people are prone to react defensively or antagonize anyone who does not fit in with their personal viewpoint. However, as I have said on numerous platforms, there is not a person alive that truly understands the nature of time, space, the universe and the human mind.

Dai and Anne, the names I have used for them, were interviewed 46 times through 2016 to 2017, separately and as a couple. The account is in their words. I have edited out my questioning and reformed both testimonies chronologically to give you a better understanding of the events. As per my style (*A most haunted house, Ghost sex: The Violation*) the account is presented as an interview. Paranormal research, as so many forget, should be focused on the witness and clarifying details of the account. I have questioned and re-questioned, cross-examining from different perspectives and avenues to ensure that the testimony is accurate and consistent.

This is a scrupulously detailed account to bring you as close to the events and the people involved as possible. The more information you have, the more you can visualise the house and the events that happened there. Dai and Anne will become more than just characters in a book, but real breathing people enduring a horrific nightmare.

At the end of their testimony, you will find the 2014 version of *A most haunted house* in its original format for new readers to gain a complete overview of the events of the house, and for returning readers to reinvestigate. You may have before you one of the most complete and unique paranormal accounts regarding hauntings in UK history. Furthermore, regardless of the obstacle that no permission has been granted or will be granted from the owners of the house (*including an attempt by a commissioned production team for Channel 4 to investigate*), I have included at the end of this book various hypotheses analysing what could be behind the haunting from the rational to the psychological to the abstruse. These will, of course, just be assumptions until a time when the house is available for a thorough and prolonged investigation.

I ask sceptics and believers alike to push away any preconceived notions which you have on the subject and investigate with an open mind what lurks behind this unassuming house in

Haverfordwest, Pembrokeshire. It is difficult for me not to compare this event to my own personal account, but Dai, Anne and I will only do so if it is necessary to the detailing of their account. What we do have to remember is that there are events happening in homes across the world that defy belief, events which are ignored and are conceivably and tragically extinguishing lives. For everyone like myself that has escaped these damnable forces, there are many, I am sure, who have dismally succumbed to the abyss.

You are now part of this, as a reader, and it is up to us to review and scrutinise the following information and evaluate as a collective. Let us try to make sense of what is happening at this house.

Let us step inside the Horror of Haverfordwest…

GL Davies

July 2017

Dwelling

The oldest and strongest emotion of mankind is fear, and the oldest and strongest kind of fear is fear of the unknown.
HP Lovecraft

Dai and Anne first supplied me with the evidence I requested to prove they had once lived in that incomprehensible house so that I knew I was not dealing with hoaxers. Verification confirmed that they had lived there from late 1989 to early 1991, 15 months in total.

Both had been born in Pembrokeshire in the early to mid-1960s, with Dai being three years older than Anne. They married in 1987. In 1989, the time the account begins, Dai worked as a driver for a large local company and Anne was a barmaid for a local Haverfordwest pub. Neither, at the time this account is set, had children, but did so in later years.

These were friendly and very down-to-earth people. Dai, a hard-working Pembrokeshire man, enjoys time with his family and working on his cars; while Anne was open, genuine and her love of her family evident in the pictures of them which adorned every available space on the walls of the house. They both have worked hard all their lives, and breaks abroad each year with their tribe is what they strive towards. While interviewing alone and as a couple, they never contradicted their story nor tried to over sensationalise. As with most genuine witnesses, there is also an initial slight apprehension when they tell their story to a stranger, for they feel that the experience of what they perceive to be real will be discredited and derided. This is part of the preliminary feeling-out process, but soon the three of us grew comfortable and trusting in each other's company. Apart from that unease during early interview sessions, their body language, micro expressions and verbal use of language never hinted at falsely presented evidence in their testimonial or that they were holding back crucial information. I am confident that their testimonial is as accurate and detailed as can be nearly thirty years on.

As for the motives for their recounting, they wish to find closure, they wish to share and they wish to find answers. They refused any monetary reward or compensation for their time. Proceeds from this book will be placed in a fund in the hope that one day the house could be purchased for scientific evaluation and investigation. This is their experience, in their own words, of what they believe happened in that house in Haverfordwest.

Anne: I would say that I did believe in the paranormal before living at the house. Pretty much everyone I knew had a story or knew of someone that had experienced something. My nan used to tell us stories about the Waterston Lady, a ghost that prowled the road just outside of Neyland, and of a house she lived in where the ghost would stroke her hair in the night or could be heard crying in the dining room. I heard about the spirit of a boy dressed as a sailor at a well-known pub which was also in Neyland. You know ghost stories from other people. I could probably tell you a hundred stories.

I have gone to psychic mediums with the girls, and half of me think they are making it up and other times they have had direct messages for my friends, and it leaves them in tears, things that they could not have known. One of my friends, in fact, was a huge believer in it and she introduced us to someone who came to the house at the time to help stop it. It seems that there is so much of it going on that there has to be something to it. I can't remember anything vivid before moving into the house and nothing since, just the odd nightmare that I am still living there. Nightmares were a huge part of what happened and I still have them. My daughter is certain her and her friends saw the Black Nun of Llangrannog, but I think everyone that has stayed there has claimed to see her; the Black Nun is more of an urban myth to scare the kids, I think.

Dai: Never really believed before Haverfordwest. Living in Pembrokeshire you can see some strange things in the sky with the military bases and all. I remember the late seventies, hearing and reading about all the UFO sightings but I never saw anything. The only thing I can remember was my mother telling me about how a lady that ran the chip shop had used to live in our house where I grew up in before we did and after the old lady died peculiar things happened in our house when we were young. Nothing bad, just windows opening, the smell of cleaning, the smell of beeswax, old-fashioned. Our clothes would be folded up overnight. Mum swore when she was in bed one night that she heard the crockery in the sink as if someone was washing up. Just nice things really. Like the old lady was helping Mum as it was just her on her own raising us kids. I can't remember anything from that time, and soon as me and my sisters were old enough it all stopped. Actually, I think it stopped the time Mum met my stepdad, so I would have been around four or five. Yeah, it's like as soon as Mum had support the old lady's ghost moved on. My sisters don't remember anything either, but Mum swore it happened. If it was real then fair enough as it was a helpful and a good presence, nothing at all like what happened in Haverfordwest.

Anne: About a year ago I was in work and the girls there were talking about this book about a haunted house in Haverfordwest. It had become quite the game of people guessing and so many were convinced they knew where it was, but deep down I knew it had to be the house we lived in. I would say our old house but it never felt like our house, so I just call it "the house". I found the book and within a few pages of reading knew it was the same place.

Dai: Anne had gotten this book and she would read parts out to me and I knew it was the house we lived in Haverfordwest. I knew what happened in that book was true because it happened to us. We had never told anyone in detail about it. Our family and close friends thought we sold the house and moved on because it nearly split us up, and we had decided on a fresh start. That is true, but obviously there was more to it than that.

Anne: There was so much that happened to us, but at the same time very different from the book. Maybe it was because we were there longer, I don't know. Maybe different people see and experience different things.

Dai: When Anne read to me the description of the house there was no doubt about it. The only thing different was that the attic conversion was not there when we were. It was just a small room back then. Not made of wood but stone like the rest of the house.

Anne: When we bought the house, the layout was the same as described in the book. You would enter through the front door on to a very small porch, which had a door that would lead straight into the living room. There was one window on the right that looked into the street and a big red brick fireplace in front of you. The room was separated by a stone arch that led to a dining area. On the far wall of the dining room was the door to the bathroom and the kitchen which led to the garden. On the left of the dining room was the stairs which led to a small landing. On the landing in front of you was a small bedroom that overlooked the street, and then to the left a master bedroom, and behind and to the left another small room which had no window at all.

Dai: It was a good-sized house for the two of us starting out. It had been well kept and needed little work inside. The garden, however, was a jungle. There was no decking then, just a small strip of grass, stone wall and steps then led to the main stretch of the garden or what would become the lawn. The grass back there was like a field. It was waist high in bits with brambles everywhere. I had never seen so many brambles in my life, thick and sharp like barbed wire.

Anne: We had decided we were going to buy, house prices

were going up and up, and we both felt that we were going nowhere paying rent. Dai's job was very well paid and I was full time at a pub in Haverfordwest, and I had a bit of money left to me after my grandmother died. We were not from Haverfordwest originally, from south of the county, but we both worked there and we began looking for a property to buy.

Dai: Anne saw it advertised in the *Western Telegraph* and it was affordable within our budget. Her friend from Milford had gone out with a lad whose dad lived there and said it was a nice enough house, but had only been there a few times as the boyfriend worked away mainly and only came home to check on his dad who was ill. You know, 'on his way out' ill.

Anne: I saw it in the paper and I mentioned it to my friend and she said it seemed nice enough. The man who lived there, her ex-boyfriend's dad, had died earlier in the year and the house was up for sale.

Dai: We viewed it several times and I liked it, typical terraced Haverfordwest house that you drive by a hundred times and never notice. Small looking from the front but stretched way back. The house was built in the late 1890s and used to be a large family house that was made into two smaller houses in the 50s. After all the awful stuff happened there and we left, I went through the deeds and parish records and there was nothing unusual other than a lot of people had lived there. Apart from the old man before us, no one had died there since the 1950s and little was known about whom it was that died there. You ask if I had any strange feelings on first entering the house when viewing it but none at all. I had no reason to at that time.

Anne: We put in an offer and snapped it up quickly. We had the keys on 6th November 1989. I was so happy. Dai and I had been seeing each other for seven years, married for over two and to finally buy a house together and then have kids. I did not feel anything strange at all when we first started looking at the house and when we got the keys. Was just a bit stuffy and needed a good clear out and paint.

Dai: I was happy. It was closer to work for both of us and it was a solid house. Solid as in – hardly any work needed doing, it was safe, and someone had looked after the place for the old man when he was there. As I said the garden needed work and the upstairs spare room was a strange one which I planned to put a skylight into but we just used it as storage. At the time, I just thought it must have been used as an attic storage space.

Anne: We had a paint party with some of our friends and spruced the place up. The original colour was very drab, very old-fashioned and old wallpaper up to the stairs and landing which we pulled down and painted instead. We stayed at Dai's mum's while we were painting and decorating and sorting out the odd little jobs. We had little to move in as it was mainly gifted from our family. Nice stuff from our elderly relatives, new sofa from Dai's mum and dad, and we picked up the little things as we went along. No online shopping back then. If you wanted something you had to find it and either hope they delivered or you borrowed a van.

Dai: We had the keys 6th November and I think we officially moved in on 18th November, which was a Saturday if I'm correct. It was definitely a Saturday morning as I was off from work and I remember borrowing my brother's strimmer, shears and saw to attack the garden. We had not rented our TV, yet, it seems strange saying that we would rent a TV so no *Grandstand* [Saturday sports program] for me to watch so I was motivated to tackle the garden.

Anne: I was running a shift that Saturday and I got home around four just before it started getting dark. I will never forget the look on Dai's face when I got home.

Dai: I had been strimming most of the day. It was a fresh, sunny winter's day, but that time of year daylight is against you so I strimmed the small lawn at the front of the garden and started to chop down the brambles, and gathered everything to the left of the garden. It was a long garden with two oak trees at the end in each corner and behind a tall brick wall of around ten feet. And behind that again, a disused lane that was filled with brambles and bushes. And behind that another tall wall that fenced off a field that was overgrown with the odd roof or frame from sheds poking through. I think that back area had once been an allotment back in the day. I had big plans for the garden. I like pottering around outside, keeping busy, and I planned to put a shed at the bottom which I would use as a workshop. I like tinkering and fixing things. When I cleared all the way to the back of the garden I came across the remains of an old structure. I assumed it to be a shed. There were bits of rotten wood and broken glass all at the back. I thought, I'm here now, quick Rollie, and let's get this cleared. I was planning a bonfire the following day so I would burn the wood too. I got picking up the wood and getting the glass in the wheelbarrow when I noticed at first something I thought was lots of seashells. I bent down and looked and it was lots of little bones, fragments. I wasn't worried as I thought maybe it had been an outhouse for chickens from back in the day. I grabbed my trowel and began scraping at the top soil, and what I found shocked me that I actually took a few steps back.

Anne: Dai is a typical man. He had a plan, just gets on with it. When I got home I couldn't believe how much he had cleared. It was wonderful as it gave me an idea of what potential we had out there. I had plans of a pond and a bench, flowerbeds and maybe a patio. Dai was just stood there staring at the ground. I called over to him a few times to say how busy he had been and if he wanted a cuppa, but he just stood there. I walked over to him and I touched his arm, and I startled him and he gave out an awful yell. He even cursed. I had never seen him look so on edge. I looked down and I gave a little gasp, it was awful.

Dai: As I had been scraping the top soil I kept uncovering more and more bones, not chicken bones at all. I don't know how many cat and dog skulls I unearthed. I don't mean one or two either – I mean dozens. The more I scraped and dug the more I found. Dozens of remains of cats and dogs. I thought maybe I had dug up an old pet cemetery, but all the skulls had been placed together. I had no idea why someone would do this. It was not the ideal thing to discover on your first day in your new home. It really spooked me but compared to what was to come this was nothing.

Creation

Life is as dear to a mute creature as it is to man. Just as one wants happiness and fears pain, just as one wants to live and not die, so do other creatures.
Dalai Lama

The garden, to me, represented the terror that was lurking inside the house. Untameable and relentless, brambles clawing and suffocating, its cruel canes throttling, ripping anything that dared take root near its domain. Dai's need to harness the garden to his and Anne's design would be a constant battle as nature would claim back any inch not enslaved to man's sovereignty, much like the entity would inside the house. The entity would seep and soak into everything, the walls and the furniture, food would spoil and clothes rot as it made its eventual slithering deep into our souls to feed. It would spread like a putrid and unfeeling virus, its acidic poison corroding veins and organs like the plagues of old.

Dai's macabre discovery was a grotesque example of unbelievable cruelty. Had someone killed these animals? Had they been family pets or strays, and why had their heads been collected and placed together? My affection for animals juxtaposed with flashes in my mind of their suffering caused me to become queasy as they told me of that first cold day in November. I visualised Dai stood hunched staring down as the winter sun dipped behind the house, his breath cold in the air, his shadow long as he tried to make sense of the grizzly find beneath him.

I asked if they had taken any pictures; but unlike today where we can take a high-resolution picture or video on our mobile phones, they would have had to use a camera which they confirmed they did not have at that time. Pictures of animal remains would not prove the inexplicable events that would take place inside but I contained an unnatural desire to see the excavation. Was it part of a ritual, a sacrifice perhaps with someone working to appease or attract the malevolence that prowled inside the house? Or was it just some sadistic coincidence?

Dai: Looking back maybe I should have called the police but the bones were decades old. At least it wasn't some old Native American burial ground. I think if the remains had been recent with bits of fur or flesh on them maybe I would have called them but it was an old burial site that had been there for who knows how long. Anne was really upset as there were over 25 skulls so I told her that a pet cemetery had probably been exhumed and all the bodies placed here out of the way, and then a shed had been built on top of it and it had just become forgotten. As shocking as it was I didn't think there was a need to become hysterical.

Anne: It was horrible but Dai said it was just an old pet cemetery and nothing to worry about, even though he looked pale after he dug it up. I remember him shovelling the bones into a builder's rubble bag and it just got tipped at the landfill. Things that happened back there later I would certainly say were linked to the grave as well as some of the visions and nightmares I had, but I will get to that in a bit.

Dai: We had fish and chip supper that night and I would say the garden had affected our mood. Anne kept asking what if the old man that had lived here before had been a devil worshipper or serial killer. I just laughed at her. Haverfordwest is not known for its cults and murderers. It's a small town, obviously even smaller back then but there had been that one guy, the Bullseye Guy [Bullseye *was an ITV game show which was a mixture of darts and general knowledge hosted by comedian Jim Bowen*], what was his name? Cooper? He was jailed for all those murders and rape. [*John William Cooper, born 3 September 1944, is a serial killer and* *diagnosed psychopath from Milford Haven, Pembrokeshire. On 26 May 2011, he was given four life sentences for the 1985 double murder of a brother and sister Richard and Helen Thomas, and the 1989 double murder of Peter and Gwenda Dixon. Cooper was also sentenced for the rape of a 16-year-old girl and a sexual assault on a 15-year-old girl, both carried out at gunpoint, in March 1996, in woodland behind the Mount Estate, Milford Haven. He had appeared as a contestant on* Bullseye *in May 1989.*] Apart from him it's been quiet in Pembrokeshire and I didn't suspect that the old man that lived here before us was a crazed lunatic.

Anne: I will admit that it played on my mind. I thought, what if there are bodies, you know, people bodies in the garden? Dai said I was being stupid. We had a takeaway, I think it would have been Pablo's Chippy, and we started to put the house together, finding homes for stuff. Reminiscing at how the house was back then to how things are now, it's a world apart. Things were so simple back then. No fancy gadgets. Our phone line had not been installed yet and if I wanted to call my mum or my friends I had to use the phone in the pub or the phone box. We didn't even have a TV until the following week, and even then, it was only four channels. Satellite TV was starting to become more popular but we didn't bother with that for years later. I was thinking as we ate that I would call my friend from Milford the next day from the pub's phone and just double check that her ex-boyfriend's dad had not been a nutter.

Dai: We locked up and we went to bed. We had pretty much put everything away and it had been a productive day.

Anne: It is always strange sleeping in a new house for the first time. It takes a bit of getting used to. The house noises, pipes, roof creaking, occasional traffic outside, but the bedroom was a nice size and we had a very comfortable bed, and I remember falling asleep quickly after a day of work and an evening tidying up.

Dai: I fell asleep and something woke me up and all I could hear is a bloody dog barking, not a small dog bark either but a big dog with a big bark. It was pitch black in the bedroom and I was disorientated as it was my first night there. I turned on the light and it was just gone two. I thought, "Where the hell is that dog barking?" I got out of bed and looked out of the window and the street was quiet and deserted and I could see nothing by the house, not anything the streetlight would shed light on. I went on the landing and pressed my ear against the wall to check if it was coming from next door. The walls of these houses are thick, I mean a few feet thick, solid stone and I heard nothing, so I went back into the bedroom and listened to the other wall and again nothing but yet I could hear this dog barking as loud as you like.

Anne: I slept through it all. I didn't even hear Dai get up.

Dai: I went downstairs and all the time it's bark, bark, bark and I was getting very irritable with it. It had to be coming from the back; maybe one of the neighbours kept their dog in the back. I had seen nothing while I had been working the garden earlier in the day. That's not to say there wasn't a dog. I just hadn't seen it. I made my way into the kitchen and it was so loud, so I knew it was coming from the back of the house. I grabbed my torch and opened the kitchen back door to the garden and it was incredibly loud at this stage. I thought, surely, other people are up. It was going through me; it was non-stop. I got on to the small lawn and walked up the steps and shone the torch down the garden and I'm not sure what I saw. Maybe I was tired. I was definitely awake and it wasn't a dream but as I shone the torch I saw a black shadow right in the middle of the garden, where I had been clearing. It was so strange as the shadow was so clear but the torch still lit the area behind it.

The shadow was featureless, it did not have eyes for instance, and it was just a black see-through shadow. The barking suddenly stopped and this shape, yes it was shaped like a large dog, just floated, more like glided to the back of the garden and I can't really explain it but the shadow melted into one of the tree trunks at the back of the garden. It just vanished. I walked up to the back of the garden and I will admit I was cautious as I had no idea what I had just seen. There was nothing in the garden that could have cast a shadow like that, trust me; I tried many times to recreate what I saw. I shone my torch this way and that, I retraced my steps from the kitchen and back outside and still there was nothing.

I know people will say, well maybe you were tired and you just saw a dog or animal or maybe the shadow was from another light source, but it was pitch black out there and apart from my torch there was no other light. You might think, well how can you hinge your paranormal account on this but you had to see it. It was so strange.

Anne: Dai was quiet the next morning. I asked him if he was OK and he said he had not slept well, and had I heard the damn dog barking? I said I heard nothing; in fact, I slept like a log. It wasn't until things started to get weirder later that he told me of the shadow in the garden, but at that time so much was happening that it seemed the least of our problems. I wish he had told me more as the night after I had a very strange experience too.

Dai: What was I to tell her? She was upset enough at the bone collection at the back of the garden without her thinking I had gone mad and was chasing imaginary dogs in the middle of the night.

Anne: That day in work I phoned my friend in Milford and asked her about the house and the old man that lived there. She said she had been seeing this man's son years before and not really got to know the dad but he seemed a nice man. She had said that he had a lung condition of sorts and was terminally ill. He was pretty much bedridden and had a nurse come to the house to look after him. The son was pleasant enough but it was a long-distance thing that every time he came to Pembrokeshire he would stay with his dad, do some bits and bobs for him and then see her. He desperately wanted to put his dad into a care home but his father just wanted to stay at home. She said she was no longer in contact with the son as he had a woman in every port so to speak and she had caught him out.

I told her about what Dai found in the back of the garden and she doubted it had anything to do with the men that lived there. She told me that they didn't have any pets, the old man was too ill to move and the son didn't seem the type in her opinion, but she said maybe she was wrong. She said maybe the place had been an old pet shop or veterinary centre in the past. I hadn't thought of anything like that. I knew there was an abattoir in Haverfordwest but nothing that should be killing cats and dogs. I thought about her explanation and I settled on it.

Dai: I have no idea what the thing, the shadow in the garden was; could it have been something to do with the grave, maybe? I don't know for sure. Anne said that maybe it had been a pet shop or a vet. She even said it might have been a foreign restaurant. I know that sounds daft but can you remember the restaurant in Haverfordwest that was closed when they found the Alsatian's head in the bins out back and dead cats in the freezer? I'm thinking between stories of murderers, dead animals in restaurants and haunted houses that the Pembrokeshire tourist board won't be too thrilled with us, but it would make sense? During my research into the house, I never found anything that proved that any of those things were at that location or even nearby but maybe way back there was.

Anne: I didn't know about Dai's encounter in the garden on night one, and my friend's theory had put my mind to rest. I told Dai and he seemed happy with that but he was distant all day. I just thought he was tired. It had been a busy weekend and he had work again the next day.

After my shift at the pub, I remember having a bath and thinking it was cold in that bathroom and checking the radiators which were on full. I moaned to Dai about it and he said the heating was fine and to just be quicker getting in and out of the bath.

Dai made his lunch for the next day and we headed up to bed. We weren't ones for reading before bed and pretty much went to sleep. That night I had one of the worst dreams I have ever had. It was an awful nightmare. I remember it as if it was last night. I can still see it today, all this time later. I was so upset that I woke up crying. I cried at Dai, I cried at work and I cried on the phone at work to my mum. I know that dreams aren't paranormal but with everything that was to come that I really think something then was already trying to get in my head. I was told later that these things can communicate to you through dreams or nightmares, through images and visions.

In my dream, I was sat in the living room, the living room of the house, but where the arch is now was a wall and a door. The house looked shabby and the walls painted a drab grey with bits peeling away. The red brick fireplace was lit and the flames were high. There looked to be an old-fashioned metal iron and a kettle on the slate hearth. The wall above the fireplace was black from smoke and there was an awful smell. I can't ever remember smelling in a dream before, but something was making me feel so sick. I read that real smells in real life can affect dreams but nothing we had in the house would smell so bad; it was a rotting smell. We had a dead rat once in the pub that ate poison and died under the floorboards, and that sickly smell of decay took weeks to shift. That was what the smell was like.

I felt anxious as I thought I was sat too close to the fire. The room was dark but there was sunlight coming in through slats behind me. I couldn't turn to see but beams of light were slicing up the room, and in the light, you could see the smoke drifting around the room. I could see through the open door into the kitchen, which seemed to be wider than it is now and there was a woman. I could only see the back of her and she was wearing a brown dress, down to her feet, baggy and unshapely. She had long greasy grey hair worn as a ponytail down to the small of her back.

The kitchen was nothing like it was now and there was no glass door at the back. The woman seemed to be leaning over a stove or something that was steaming. I could sense or feel something on my lap and I looked down and there was a cat. This is so awful it makes me so upset, even telling you all this time later. I need a quick break, if that is OK?

(A brief interval is taken while Anne composes herself.)

Thank you, this is rough and please don't think anything less of me but it was a nightmare and nothing I would ever, ever do. You must understand that I would never harm anything. I love animals; I ask Dai to put spiders outside for me and not to hurt them. I didn't even want to put rat poison down at the pub as I felt sorry for the rat if it had babies to look after. Silly I know but I could never hurt anything. Before I carry on please know that of me. This is not something I would ever think of doing.

I looked down and there is a cat on my lap. It's twitching a little bit, its fur, its skin from its paws to its shoulders has been pulled back, you can see the muscle and bones and there is blood all over my lap. Its tail has been broken or hacked off and there is just a jagged bone jutting out. Someone has wrapped a cloth around its head. The cloth has steam coming off it. The cat is suffocating and has hardly any strength, just a little twitch and then it soils itself all over my lap and it is still. The cat is still but there are little bumps moving under its midsection, like unborn kittens desperate to be born. I just wanted to wake up, I just wanted to scream. Why would someone do this? Why would I dream this? Someone had poured boiling water on a rag and tied it over the cat's face and skinned its legs and cut off its tail. I looked up and the old lady was right in front of me screaming at me. Her face old and wrinkled, teeth black, skin like yellow flypaper, she screamed: *"Get out!"*

Dai: Anne woke me, she was screaming so loudly. If anyone had heard they would have thought there was a murder taking place. One night it's a dog barking and now Anne was screaming. I was a nervous wreck. I turned on the light and Anne was stood in the corner of the room just screaming. She was still asleep. They say not to wake anyone up who is sleepwalking but the screaming was piercing. We would have had the police around I'm sure if she had not stopped. I tried calling her name but nothing, so I had to shake her shoulders.

Anne: I woke up and Dai was shaking me and shouting at me and I had no idea where I was. I didn't know I had been screaming and I had no idea how I got to the other side of the room. I sat on the bed shaking, and I cried and sobbed all night. I had no idea what was happening. A dream like that, so vivid, you can't shake off easily. I never suspected at that time it was the house. I thought with what we found at the back of the garden and my chat with my friend that it had all been playing in my mind. As horrible as it was that was all it was, right? That was the first night like that. There would be a lot more. So many that I started a journal. I never imagined that I could see such terrible things in all my life but a dream is one thing but seeing it, in reality, nothing can prepare you for it.

Occupation

They say that shadows of deceased ghosts
Do haunt the houses and the graves about,
Of such whose life's lamp went untimely out,
Delighting still in their forsaken hosts.
Joshua Sylvester

Anne broke down many times during her account of her nightmare. Her eyes welled up as she visualised the imagery of the dream, a nightmare that had haunted her for nearly thirty years and was still as shocking to her now as it had been all those years back.

It is not uncommon for deeply traumatic images or stressful experiences, even dreams, to be stored in the brain and replayed. Anne admitted that she would have involuntary flashbacks of the monstrous images of animal cruelty from this dream and from other nightmares that would happen later. In an explicit flashback, the person is involuntarily transported back in time. To the person, it does not seem so. What they experience is being experienced as if it were happening in the present. Her flashbacks and remembrance were twofold. It was a flashback from thirty years ago that was a dream that seemed to take her back further in time again.

Was she a witness or the perpetrator of the atrocity? The image of the suffering of the cat made me physically ill and dwells within me now unleashing sadness and anger, even if we can classify it merely as a dream. Anne's reaction convinced me that there was much more to this – and there would be, just as harrowing and just as traumatic as that initial vision.

Based on the information that she recalled in the dream it appears that the dress and items which she saw would have placed the house anywhere from its construction in 1890 to at least 1920, if not further forward again. The paint used at the time would have been mixed with lead, and subsequent research would loosely estimate – allowing that the decay described on the walls was at least ten years after the construction was complete – it would have been painted in 1890. The grey described on the walls was a very popular colour at the time and it is feasible that this was a French grey which was an affordable option then. Had Anne's vision been one of the house at the turn of the twentieth century or had her mind merely conjured up through her own conscious and subconscious a portrayal of what the house would have been like 90 years previous? One can run wild with speculation of a vivid imagination, time travel and even past life recognition, and these are ideas that we will explore later.

The old woman, angry and seething, was an ominous character in all of this. The mere mention of an old lady twisted a tight knot in the pit of my stomach. I felt I knew this woman. Was she the one heard screaming at me that dreadful night that perpetrated the beginning of the end of my relationship as I begged for peace detailed in *A most haunted house*? This was a figure that needed further enquiry. Was she the link between my own account and this new testimony? My mind began to race at the possibility of tying together the two accounts.

What had Dai witnessed in the garden that night? A rational man had succumbed to confusion and near panic. Whatever he had seen had worried him.

The ghosts of animals, in what we are to assume has no rational explanation, is not uncommon. Black dogs are typical in British folklore and have the ability to vanish, shapeshift and pass through solid objects. Alan Murdie's study into the Black Dog sightings infers witnesses to the black dog phenomena are usually awake, alert and travelling somewhere. Pembrokeshire has its own Devil Hound folklore: a black demon-eyed beast often seen prowling around Llanmill and Narberth with reports covered at length at The Paranormal Chronicles. Black dogs are said to be the harbinger of death or misfortune, so what had Dai seen?

Had his excavation of the remains disturbed the tortured souls of pets, and did the shape represent the collective souls of all the creatures or just one of the animals laid to rest there? Where had these animals come from and was there a connection to Anne's dream?

Dai, like I, had gone through the history of the house at length and found nothing to establish why the house was the epicentre of a dark and cruel presence. He had investigated if a vet, pet cemetery, pet shop, or a restaurant had existed in the vicinity or any other establishment that could shed light on the animal remains or even the activity at the house. There was nothing listed that could confirm the theory. The only intriguing evidence present was that a number of people had lived in that house. Dozens of people had lived there from 1989 to the present, and compared to other houses in the area was vastly high in correlation. From 1890 to 1950 the information was vague and the house was listed as the property of an investment entrepreneur from London, and local records list the house as empty for long stretches of time. Had people lived there off the record? Had the property owner rented his house privately to family or acquaintances? The house was shrouded in mystery. Had someone been hiding something or someone?

The testimony was still in its infancy and there was a great deal still to discover, things you will hope you never encounter.

Anne: Dai had to go to work the next morning and I begged him not to go. I had never had a dream or a nightmare that vivid before and it was as traumatic as if it had been real. Dai had been quiet all weekend and I thought he must be tired and fed up.

Dai: It had not been the best of starts in our new home. I was tired and had two nights of little to no sleep and had seen who knows what in the garden, and, along with mass animal remains,

Anne screaming and sleepwalking. I just put it down to stress. We do drink socially. I like a pint on weekends but we had never done drugs not even a puff of weed, so we weren't drunk or high or anything like that. At this stage, I didn't even think there was something supernatural happening. You rationalise, don't you? Maybe it had been a real dog in the garden, maybe it was a shadow of something I didn't see as I was tired, maybe it was a prank. Heck, maybe I was the one sleepwalking.

Anne, which was not like her, was beside herself. She was sobbing up until I left that Monday morning. I didn't know what to say. She had a nightmare and a horrific one at that. We all get nightmares, we all get stressed and we all have bad dreams. Sleepwalking was new, but it had been a stressful weekend in hindsight, so I told her to go back to bed and let it go. I said to go get some sleep and by the evening she will be alright again.

Anne: It is hard to shake something like that off. I wasn't working that day and I didn't want to stay in the house on my own. I don't want to lie and say I knew the house was wrong, that something was happening there; but I just didn't feel comfortable being there alone. If there were bones in the garden then who knows what else was hiding behind a wall, or a cupboard. I just wasn't thinking straight. I went to work and said I had forgotten to sort out a few things for the delivery and went in and used the phone.

I had to hide out in the back as I was shaking. People would have thought someone had died the way I was carrying on. I spoke to my mum, cried at her, spoke to my friend, cried at her and both told me it was just a nightmare and Mum said to have a sherry to take the edge off. It was good to get it off my chest and a sherry did help a little.

Dai: I got home that evening and Anne still wasn't right, but she seemed better than she had in the morning. I was shattered but I told her to get her coat and let's go for pint and food at a pub... Can I say which one? It was by the cinema. She was happy to get out and once we were in the pub having a drink and some food, other people around and music playing she did cheer up.

Anne: Dai took me out for pub grub and we talked about the weekend and how strange it had been. He still hadn't told me about the dog yet and we just put it down to stress. We started planning again and we were excited as we were getting a new TV on the weekend and a few days after that a phone line, so I had a lifeline to my family and friends.

Dai: She seemed better after that. We went home and nothing happened for a while as far as I remember.

Anne: We were trying for children so we went home and had some time to ourselves and nothing strange happened that night. I didn't have a weird dream that night and Dai slept like a log. The next day we were back more to our usual selves, but I still found myself thinking of the dream but tried to busy myself. The feeling I had reminded me of when my nan died. I went to see her in the hospital; it was a few hours before the end and she was hooked up to all these pipes and tubes and the family was there. They say that death is peaceful but the panic in my nan's eyes was terrifying. She looked at me with desperate eyes and when my mum told me to hold her hand, she grabbed it and squeezed it, not lovingly but as if she was scared. This woman had been so full of life and now she was about to take her last breath and she didn't want to go. That look in her eyes – haunted me, for so long. Thankfully I saw her at the chapel of rest and they do such a good job, don't they? She looked, well, healthy. She looked like she was just asleep and would wake up at any moment and that helped me think of her at rest, but now and again that look of hers would pop into my head and worry me, scare me.

Dai: We got the TV which pleased me as I had been missing the football and sport, and then the phone line and that kept Anne on it. She was glued to it, but I didn't mind as she paid the phone bill.

Anne: Christmas of 1989 was around the corner and I like the decorations up nice and early, but Dai always moans that we should wait till he gets the tree. He had a friend who got trees for him and we got it that year around the 8th December. I remember as it was the anniversary of John Lennon's murder. I am a huge Beatle fan, it broke my heart the day he was killed. Still, I was so excited to put up the tree and the decks [decorations].

Dai: Nothing had happened at all since that first weekend but as soon as the decks went up little things started to happen. Nothing as strange as animal shadows and dreams, but little things. Now back then we weren't educated on the paranormal like now it's all over TV, in movies, everywhere, so we didn't know what was happening, while now with all the info online and on TV we would have known something odd was happening.

Anne: That night we got the house looking fantastic. It looked so magical with the big red brick mantelpiece and the arch separating the living and dining room. Before bed, I went into the bathroom for a pee and it was freezing in there. You could literally feel the divide of warmth and cold as you walked through the door. The radiator was on and the window was closed, so I went upstairs and asked Dai to get up and have a look.

Dai: I was already in bed and to be honest I didn't want to get up to just see how cold it was. She had mentioned it before and I thought there must be a draught or something. She nagged me to go down so I did. It was cold out, it was just above freezing, and the pavement was a little icy, but inside it was nice and toasty. She was right though, the bathroom was freezing, way below I would say, you could see your breath and there was a slight frost on the shower door. The heating was on to the degree that it would burn your hand if you kept it on there for too long and the window was closed. It was so strange. I looked around the bathroom to see if there was an obvious cause, you know, like a crack in the ceiling, maybe a hole in the wall behind the toilet, something like that. I couldn't see anything so I thought that maybe behind the panelling on the bath… maybe there was something back there causing the cold, even though that wall was connected to the kitchen. I told Anne I would look at it on the weekend.

Anne: The next night was colder outside but not in the bathroom. Dai had no explanation for it.

Dai: The cold in there would come and go. At first, I thought it was something to do with a draught coming from outside but even on warmer nights, the temperature would drop in there. It was always between 11 and 11:30 too when it happened at night, but we didn't start to look at all this and start to look for patterns until a few months later.

Anne: On Christmas morning, we got up early as we were going to stay at my mum's in Neyland and we wanted a few hours to ourselves. We had spent the evening in the pub and had a great night. I was working behind the bar and Dai and his workmates all came in for a festive tipple. It was such a good night. We woke up the next morning and there was this awful, terrible smell.

Dai: The smell? God, it was vile. I joked to Anne that maybe she had drunk too much the night before and had an accident in the bed.

Anne: It was terrible. I went downstairs and it was everywhere. I checked the toilet as I thought maybe Dai hadn't flushed from the night before as we had quite a few drinks. He was cross that I could even think it was him. He even went outside to see if it was something out there.

Dai: I can't fully compare the stench to anything I know. It was a mixture of silage or worse, and then it would smell like onions, sometimes something burning, but all mingled together. It was suffocating. On Christmas morning, we had all the windows open and still we couldn't get rid of it. We planned on a cheeky Christmas breakfast but that smell just turned us right off.

Anne: I'm not sure how to describe it but like someone had gone to the toilet in the middle of the room but there was also an eggy smell and burning food or something. We thought maybe something had got into the house and died. It was really disgusting. We left early for our mums' and we were paranoid it would be on our clothes, and we drove to Neyland with the windows open in the car. When we got back there was no smell at all.

Dai: I expected it to be rough when we got back and must sleep with all the windows open but it had gone. Anne would nag me – where did it come from, would it be back – and I would just say it could have been gas seeping from under the house, anything I could to keep her from worrying about it, but in hindsight that would worry me more if someone told me that.

Anne: As we lived in a terrace I would try and keep an eye out for the neighbours so I could be nosy and ask them about the smell. Now the house to our right, if you are facing ours from the street, well, we never saw anyone there the whole time we were there. Their house would have been part of our house in the olden days and I was always curious to have a look inside so I could see what the house would have looked like as one big house. On the other side was an old couple and they didn't speak to us at all. In fact, you could say they were rude. Dai knocked one day to see about the hedge that separated both our gardens, as he was cutting his side and he offered to do theirs, and the old man said, not today thank you, and closed the door.

Dai: I don't think they were rude. I think he was foreign as he just sounded different. Maybe they had come here after the war. Maybe they were so old that they were nervous of people as I rarely saw them come and go, and I don't think I ever saw anyone come and visit them. In hindsight, maybe they saw so many people come and go from the house that they just never bothered with anyone. I couldn't tell you or even guess if they had the same problems in their house. I guess we will never know unless someone who reads this figures out who they were and what their background was.

Anne: Before Christmas, we got a new TV and a phone, and I got Dai a new radio from that place on Swan Square called Alabaster, they used to sell and repair TVs and radios, electronics and that kind of stuff. There is a point to this as they got to know us well.

Dai: We got the TV and set up, great. We get the phone and that is set up, great. Anne buys me a radio for Christmas. Great radio, double cassettes, yep, double cassettes back then and Boxing Day I set it up and it was great. Anne would use it to tape the Top 40, which I think was on that Boxing Day even though the charts were normally on a Sunday. Anyway, she is using it more than me and she's taping songs on to the cassette. She was in the kitchen and she is playing back her tape. I don't know how many times she ejected and replayed, over and over, singing along to the songs.

I'm watching a film on TV when she comes in and says the radio is broken. I was cross because you couldn't just pause the film like you could today, plus we had only used it that day. I got up and asked her what was wrong and she said all her songs were gone. I turned the radio on and it was working. I pressed play and no sound. I took the tape out and it hadn't broken so put it back in and pressed play and thought the volume... maybe she had knocked the volume, so I turned it all the way up. All you could hear was a crackling but if you listened closely you could hear a whisper, not static but a whisper.

Anne: One minute I'm listening to my tape and the next second it's just crackling. Dai tried to fix it, and when he turned the volume up and all you could hear was this whisper. It gave me goosebumps. He was leaning into the radio, trying to make out what it was saying when the music came back on so loud that he jumped out of his skin.

Dai: It nearly killed me! I was scared witless. The tape was thirty minutes each side and I rewound the tape and played from the start, and there was no crackling and no whispering anywhere on the tape. Hardly paranormal I know as it could have just been a defective tape or radio, but the things that started to happen after that made me realise this was the start of it. You could hear whispering, not like if the song or the DJ was turned down, but an actual whisper.

Anne: A few days later I got home from the pub and Dai was stressed as the TV wasn't working, and the phone kept ringing and when he answered it, it kept hanging up. I thought maybe something was wrong with Mum, so I called her and she was fine and that everyone as far as she knew was fine. I can't remember having a 'who called me' button back then. If there was then I didn't know about it. Dai was in a mood as there was something he wanted to watch.

Dai: The TV just stopped working. I try turning it on and off and nothing. I unplug it and nothing. As I'm trying to fix it the phone keeps bloody ringing, and as soon as I answered there would be silence and then it would click and go to the dial tone. Anne goes into the kitchen and comes back with a look on her face that says, I'm going to kill her, and when I ask what was up she said the radio wasn't working.

Anne: Dai was huffing around the TV and I thought it was best to just give him some peace so went into the kitchen and turned on the radio, not too loud as I didn't want to aggravate him more than he was. I had Radio 1 on and halfway through a song it just cut out and there was a clacking sound, you know, like interference. I retuned the radio and nothing. I went through the whole FM channels and couldn't get a reception so I thought it was just that, no reception. It had a pull-out aerial and that was fully extended and pointed towards the window and still nothing, even on the other settings. It didn't matter where I was tuned, it was just this strange clacking noise. I turned it on to tape mode and pressed play and again just this clacking noise. So, I turned it off and guess what? It was still clacking! I unplugged it and still, it was doing it. I went and told Dai and he was utterly fed up.

Dai: Anne asks me to look at the radio and it is making this god-awful clacking noise, like a static. Even with the volume down and even unplugged it still made the noise. The only thing I could think was that there had been a huge electrical surge in the house or the street, and it had fried everything electronic.

Anne: Dai was trying to figure out what was going on and he was red-faced and swearing, and to make it worse the phone started to ring. I picked up the phone and had to drop it as the phone was making the clacking noise too. I hung it up and picked it back up and there was no dial tone, just – well there was a lot going on with Dai mumbling in the kitchen – but it sounded like the whisper we had heard on the radio that night.

Dai: Anne looked pale and said the phone was playing up. She said it was clacking too which made me think that maybe the radio was doing it and it was picking up in the receiver of the phone. I'm not an engineer but you look for rational explanations. I unplugged the phone and then turned off the electricity at the mains and turned it back on. Nothing worked after that, no weird noises but the TV, radio and phone were all dead. I worked with a few lads from Haverfordwest and when I saw them in work I asked if they had experienced power outages or electrical issues, and they said no. They joked that I should have just got my TV and radio from Vaughan's [a local electrical supplier] and not from the rental place.

Anne: I was off the next day so I popped down to the TV place which is where Subway is now on Castle Square and the woman in there was very apologetic, and said if I could bring it down as soon as I could then would look to repair or replace it. I brought the radio down with the receipt to the radio place on Swan Square and the man there put the radio on the counter and turned it on and it worked fine. The radio was fine and the tape played the songs I had taped. He said it may have been something to do with our electrics so he said to try again, but if happened again he would look at replacing the radio. I popped into the pub and called the phone company and the electric people, and they said they would send engineers around.

Dai: We took the TV down, and low and behold the TV works fine in the showroom. The lady was not very technically minded but said it could be our electrics but they were happy to replace the TV, in fact, she upgraded us and we ended up paying an extra couple of quid a week; good saleswoman.

Anne: The phone people and electrical people came around and everything was working fine. They replaced the handset and the phone line was working. The electrics were fine too.

Dai: We set up the TV and it works brilliantly, and the radio and phone are working well. It was so baffling. We had no idea as did the engineers, but everyone was helpful and to be honest you just want it fixed, don't you? However it's done just fix it, and as everything was working again then we were both happy.

Anne: There was a lot more of that to come but as time went on little happened that we noticed until around Easter 1990 when the activity started to pick up. Just little things at first but it was like it was building up. The things that happened were very human in some respects but I honestly don't believe the thing in the house was human at all. It plays with you, it puts you on edge, it makes you paranoid and insecure, it wants you to question your sanity.

Dai: It was messing with us. It pushes and pushes to see how much you will take. Everything up to now was like it was testing I guess or building itself up for the real damaging stuff.

Anne: It was Good Friday and I was off, as was Dai, and we had a late night. I can't exactly remember what we were up to but I think we had gone out for a few drinks or a meal, something like that as we both didn't have to be up early the next day. I got up and made my way downstairs. The stairs don't have a bannister so as you walk down you can see into the dining area as you head directly to the bathroom. The light was coming in from the front window and as I headed down I looked at the clock on the dresser to check what time it was, and it was just after ten. I went into the bathroom, had a pee and headed back out, and I did a double take as on the floor was big muddy boot marks across our nice cream carpet. I was furious as I first thought that Dai had done it and then I panicked as I thought we had been burgled but the footprints only went left to right across the carpet, wall to wall, not from the door to the living room and through the house but wall to wall. I remember panicking, like really scared someone was down there and ran upstairs shouting for Dai to wake up.

Dai: Anne burst into the bedroom shouting and it scared the life out of me. She was panicking and she was getting dressed in a hurry. She said someone was downstairs. I thought what? I jumped out of bed and headed down and couldn't see anything. I checked the kitchen and bathroom and the front door and everything was locked. There was no one in the house. She was calling down the stairs to be careful, and then she said, "How did the footprints get in the living room?" And I said, "What footprints?"

Anne: Dai was down there and I expected something to smash or Dai to start shouting at someone, but he just called up and said, what was I on about?

Dai: There was nothing at all to even consider we had an intruder. I told her to come down and see for herself.

Anne: I went down slowly as I half expected Dai to be held hostage and they were telling him what to say. Dai was stood directly under the arch that divides the living room from the dining room and he was just stood there in his pants looking tired and confused. I looked to where the boot prints had been and there was nothing. Not even a hint that someone had walked through. My heart was pounding in my chest, as I know what I saw.

Dai: She showed me where she thought she saw the boot prints and there was nothing at all. I couldn't even begin to make an excuse for her and say she had mistaken it for something else. I said maybe she had been tired or maybe she had looked at the light of the window and it made those imprint things on your eyes after you have looked at a bright light for too long. She swore they were there and she got cross saying she knew what she had seen. I got cross back and said, "Where were they then?" I told her I hadn't made them, I hadn't cleaned them up, "So where were they?"

Anne: We had a row as we were both stressed. I was convinced that I had seen them. They were big and muddy and very clear, maybe six or seven boot prints in all. Dai mocked me and said what six? What was it a giant? He said the person would have to be so tall to have a stride that long. He said I was making it up.

Dai: Yeah, I was rough on her that morning. I think that's when the cracks began to appear.

Anne: We started arguing and when you do loads of stuff comes up, you know, buried stuff. He said I didn't listen to him, and I said he was more interested in watching the bastard TV. He said I'd rather be on the phone chatting to the world than talking to him, and I said that talking and listening about sport was boring and I didn't give a hoot. And then I stopped as I saw something that just took the wind out of my sails.

Dai: We were arguing over petty stuff if I recall, but I just got so angry. I'm not a fan of confrontation and I hate it. Anne is good at it so I tend to keep my head low, even now. I was off on one and just fuming at the things she was saying. I remember saying something like if she was a bloke then I would knock her out, things I would never say, and then she just stopped and looked behind me and the colour drained from her face. I turned and I wasn't sure what I was looking at.

Anne: It was like time froze as behind Dai was our leather armchair; a lovely chair that was given to us by Dai's grandparents and the chair had an impression on the seat. Something I never noticed before and never noticed again. There was an impression like someone was sat there. I pointed to it and Dai looked at it saying what, what was I on about now?

Dai: I looked at the chair and the strangest thing was that it looked like someone was sat on it. I hadn't sat on it and Anne was nowhere near it and I watched as the impression in the chair slowly disappeared as if someone had just stood up.

Anne: It was as if someone was sat there, or had been sat there. Looking back, I imagine something sat there just enjoying us arguing like it was a spectator. To this day I have no idea where those footprints went but soon enough we would know who left them behind.

Another

Good courage in a bad affair is half of the evil overcome.
Plautus

As a researcher and investigator into all things paranormal, it is astonishing how witnesses that have had prolonged experiences make excuses for the strange events that invade their lives. Our society, as a whole, demeans such notions and places a stigma on most that openly admit to such supernatural interaction as mentally unstable, deceitful or lacking moral fibre. Why is a society so afraid of admitting that there may be more to what science can explain? Who exactly is making that collective decision on what we are comfortably allowed to believe, and what we should scorn and judge as nonsense?

Anne, thirty years removed from her experience, is open to the idea that something entirely different from us permeates our reality. She is not held up on mere superstitions or religious beliefs, but she has a knowing look when talking about the paranormal subject. She is not one to dismiss easily and like a person that has seen the horrors of war she has a stare of someone who has witnessed unfathomable things.

Dai has a distinct divergence; like myself, he knows what he saw yet part of him cannot readily accept it. Every occurrence from the house he tells with a faraway stare as if he has been forcefully made to return to the house, but he is quick to offer up explanations. This is part of his coping mechanism. It helps him distance himself from the entity as if finding rational interpretations gives him power over the living darkness.

I have interviewed numerous sceptics that distance themselves from the reality of the paranormal as they too, deep down, are terrified that maybe there are elements of this world they cannot control. Their initial demeanour is brash, confident, assured in their knowledge of science and of the world, but when invited on investigations and the lights go off, the adrenaline starts to pump and they are immersed in a world of possibility. Their defences dissolve. Fear is one emotion that unites every single person on this planet. It affects the knowledgeable and the ignorant in equal measure.

We began discussing at length a very difficult time in Dai and Anne's relationship. The house was manifesting its insidious design. It had grown in strength. It was hungry for discord, and it needed to feed.

Anne: A few weeks after the boots, I had a call from Dai's work saying that Dai had been in an accident. He had been working late nights on deliveries and we were like ships in the night since his shifts changed. I panicked as I thought he had been in a crash or something.

Dai: I was working late and it was gone ten and was pretty much dark for that time of year. I was getting out of the cab to the truck, and as I dropped down my foot hit an uneven surface and I snapped my foot. I broke my ankle clean and fractured my tibia. It hurt like hell. There was no one about and it was my right foot. I had no mobile back then and there was no phone, and I was north of the county in the middle of nowhere. I can tell you that was the longest drive home of my life. The pain was excruciating. It makes me wince now thinking of going over on my foot like that, and I sweated the whole time I drove home.

Luckily it was not a bad break and the bone did not come out of the skin or anything, but I did have to go in a cast. Work panicked as the area where I was working was supposed to be manned and have lights, plus the uneven surface, so they could not do enough for me. They gave me full pay. They even sent Anne a hamper and flowers. I was scheduled to be off for a minimum of two to three months.

Anne: Poor Dai had broken his ankle. It was a big cock-up that he had been hurt in the first place and his work was very sorry. There was an agreement that I can't discuss and it was based on that Dai did not seek legal advice or go through the union, then they would compensate him plus give him full pay.

Dai: I liked my job; I never minded going to work each day. I was on my own most days, radio on and got to drive around West Wales. The idea of sitting at home with my leg in plaster was not a great option but I was being paid so what can you do? You just try and make the most of a bad situation.

Anne: It was nice to see him more often though. I picked up extra hours in the pub, but I would see him every morning and make sure he was OK and had everything he needed for the day.

Dai: I slept downstairs for the first month I think. I was doped up on medication and I was sleeping a lot, which is probably the best way to heal. I had a pair of crutches but I struggled with them. I nearly fell and broke my damn wrist while using them. The toilet and kitchen were downstairs so it made sense to sleep down there.

Anne: A few weeks of Dai being home and I came home one evening and he is sat there, foot up and watching TV, and there is an overpowering smell in the living room, not a vile smell like before, but of perfume. Like a lavender and rose. I asked him who had been to visit and he looked at me as if I was mad; and then I asked him what had he been spraying and he looked at me and said nothing. I asked, could he smell that and he said, "What?"

Dai: Anne started nagging me about this smell. I had no idea what she was on about. I couldn't smell anything.

Anne: It was a distinct smell, like an old woman's smell. My gran used to smell of lavender but this was lavender and rose I think.

Dai: I never smelt it, so I can't comment.

Anne: One night I came home and again I smell it, so I just asked him, what was going on? Was someone coming over in the day to see him?

Dai: She asked me why someone was coming over in the day and I was not telling her about it. I said, no one. Our friends and family often visited on weekends and I had the phone if I needed anything. Anne got so paranoid that someone was coming to visit me. Then one time as I was sleeping on the settee she gave me an almighty grilling.

Anne: One night I'm in bed and I hear the phone ringing downstairs, and it's answered really quickly and I hear Dai talking to someone. I thought, it's gone two in the morning, what's happened? Has something happened to one of our family or friends, and I dashed up and went downstairs. The light was off and I turned it on expecting Dai to be sat there in the dark talking on the phone. Dai was asleep on the sofa. I asked him who it was on the phone and he just lay there so I woke him up. He was all sleepy and I asked again, "Who was on the phone?" He asked, "When?" I said, "Just now." He said he never heard the phone.

Dai: Anne started to get really strange with me. She woke me up in the middle of the night to ask me who I was talking to. She said she heard the phone ringing, and she heard me answering it. I swore to her that I hadn't and maybe she had heard the old couple next door, which to be honest was a long shot as we never heard a peep out of them. They were very quiet plus the walls were thick. I said, was it someone outside on the street or maybe she had dreamt it? She got cross with me and stormed off.

Anne: I heard the phone and I heard a man answer it. I was growing suspicious of him. I thought maybe he was seeing someone and they had called him, maybe they were drunk. I don't know but that's all I could think of. He said he didn't hear it, but it was eating me inside, and low and behold it happened the next night.

Dai: The night after, Anne wakes me up again and says she's had enough of me lying to her, and why couldn't I just respect her and tell her the truth. I asked, "The truth about what?" She said I was on the phone talking to some fancy woman who was probably drunk and threatening to reveal their affair. I did the worst thing a man could do and laughed. I told her she sounded like a nutter and she needed help. No phone had been ringing, and unless I was sleepwalking I had not touched the bloody phone. She stormed off upstairs shouting that it was over.

Anne: I ignored him the next day; I didn't fill the kettle up or sort out his food for the day. He asked me on my way out if we were OK and could we talk, and I said he could shove it up his arse, and that after I had worked my next two shifts that I would be staying at my mum's for a bit.

Dai: I pleaded with her to calm down, and I swore that nothing was going on and that I was worried about her. She is smelling perfume and hearing me talking on the phone in the middle of the night when I know nothing about these things. We have been through some tough times and I have never stopped loving her and I would never hurt her especially with another woman. I trust Anne. I know she would not do that to me either, so where all this was coming from I didn't know, even though later on, it would happen to me. I suspected maybe she was having an episode, maybe a breakdown.

Anne: That night I came home late, gone 1am, and Dai was already sleeping on the settee. I was shattered, and to be honest I had no desire to talk to him so headed up straight to bed. Now, every morning, I get out of bed and I make the bed. I am very clean and tidy, and have my little routine. I went to the bedroom and it was stinking of that perfume and the duvet was all ruffled up and hanging halfway off the bed. A pillow was on the floor. I was tired, and I was tired of this smell in the house and Dai ignoring it like it didn't exist and the phone calls and acting like I was the one who had gone mad. I knew now he was having an affair, blatant and with no respect for me whatsoever. He is at home with his woman, in our bed, under our roof and he has the cheek to say I'm making it all up. If he wanted me gone then I would go.

Dai: I was fast asleep and next thing I'm awake and she's shouting at me in the living room, the light is on and it's hurting my eyes and I have no idea what is happening. All she keeps shouting, "Who is she, who is she?" I thought, not this again. Looking back, it was awful for us both and reliving it now is not easy, especially with what happened.

Anne: I feel so ashamed now but I called him every name under the sun and told him to get out of the house. He was on one leg and where would he go at that time of night but still I threw him out. He asked to use the phone to call his brother but I… I'm so ashamed, I am so sorry for this but I hit him and he quietly hobbled out and sat in his car on the street all night. I wouldn't even let him have his car keys.

Dai: What was I to do? There was no talking to her. She was convinced that I had been having an affair. I swear on both my children's lives that I never. There was no one, not even flirting or chatting up, just Anne. I have never seen her like that. She hit me and pushed me. I just wanted out of the house.

Anne: I know now that he wasn't but I was so convinced at the time. It was like my inner voice was telling me he was. I have never acted like that before or since, but everything was pushing me to believe he was sleeping with someone else and in our bed. It was not even solid evidence. In hindsight, telling you now you probably are thinking, why did she act so irrational, but I couldn't help it. It sounds like a terrible excuse but it was almost as if it wasn't me.

Dai: The next day, I asked for the keys and she let me into the house but never said a word. I grabbed my keys and asked if we could talk, and she was silent. I had no idea what was going on. It was an uncomfortable drive to Milford Haven to stay with my brother. I told him about it, and he thought she had suffered a nervous breakdown. He even asked if she was on drugs. That maybe she had fallen in with a bad crowd at the pub. It was so unlike her.

Anne: I ignored him completely. He called and I hung up. His brother called and I hung up. His mum called and I hung up on her. Then my mum called and said this was not like Dai, and that I needed to just calm down and think about what I was throwing away.

I went to work that day and I was so numb. All I imagined was him with another woman. I imagined both naked in my bed, laughing at me. It is so wrong, but it was in my head the whole time. I was seeing them at it; things we would do together, I could see him doing to this mystery woman. I could see him saying he loved her and he would finish with me so they could get married and have children.

I was snappy with the people I worked with and the customers. One of the guys, a local called Jimmy, made a joke, saying I was on my period and I barred him from the pub after giving him a hell of a scolding. I was spinning out of control. I was full of anger and hate.

Dai: I tried calling. I spoke to her mum, my mother. Her mum said to just give her space and that she would try and calm it all down. She asked me to tell her the truth, had I been having an affair? I said of course not and she said she believed me. All I could do was wait. It was a terrible time as I wasn't working, I'm living at my brother's and I have no idea if I would ever see Anne again.

Anne: The owner of the pub asked me to take a few days off. She said I needed to sort out my home life as there had been complaints in the pub that I was causing an atmosphere and some of the patrons were going elsewhere to drink. I didn't feel like I needed a break but she told me I had to.

At home, I had stripped the bed and put on new bed sheets and duvet as I could smell her on them. I opened all the windows and cleaned the house from top to bottom as if cleaning the house would remove what had happened. No matter how much I cleaned, the smell would not go away. Mum popped over and I said, could she smell the perfume, and she was puzzled and said all she could smell was polish and bleach. It was so strong. I told her everything, and she said she didn't think Dai was having an affair at all and that maybe I was just under a lot of pressure.

It made my blood boil at the time that everyone was acting like it was my fault. I was so obsessed with it that I thought that maybe Dai was paying my family off with his settlement to get me thrown in the asylum so he could have the house with his fancy woman.

I said to Mum, "Then if I'm making it up then why does the house smell of perfume?" Why was the bed unmade? Why was Dai taking phone calls in the middle of the night and then pretending he was asleep? Mum just answered that she couldn't smell the perfume and maybe I had forgotten to make the bed that morning, and that I had dreamt the phone had been ringing, and guess what? I threw her out. I swore at her and told her she was no mother of mine and... Oh my God – maybe I should have been thrown in the asylum – as I accused her of sleeping with Dai. Crazy, I know. It sounds insane telling you this. I can't apologise enough for that. I cringe every time I think of it.

Dai: Anne's mum was a very attractive lady for her age but to seriously consider I would have an affair with her was berserk. My foot was in agony and the drugs weren't doing much for my energy levels and libido, and I just put it all down to not giving Anne enough attention. Plus she was working more hours so was tired, and also she puts a lot of pressure on herself. Then, I had the phone call.

Anne: That night I went to bed in a right state. I had been shouting and screaming since I had thrown Mum out, and I turned the volume down on the phone as I didn't want to talk to anyone. I went to bed and lay there just thinking of Dai having sex with this woman, even sleeping with my mum and it just broke my heart. One good thing was the damn smell had gone.

I lay in bed sobbing for most of the night. I woke up as I thought I heard the phone ringing and a man answer it. I was furious as Dai had obviously snuck in and was calling the woman again. I rushed out of bed and stormed downstairs and when I turned on the light there was no one there. The front door was locked and the phone was still on silent. At the time, I thought that maybe I was going mad. I sat there sobbing. What was happening to me? That was all I could think. I was mentally ill, I was going mad and I would be locked up. I remember it vividly because there was a thump upstairs like something had fallen.

I went upstairs and I couldn't see anything that had fallen off the bedside cabinet or the drawers, and I went back to bed. I turned off the light and lay there just doubting myself but also thinking that maybe Mum and Dai had snuck into the house somehow and were playing tricks on me, you know, to convince me I was not right in the head.

I was lying there when I heard a door opening. I heard the latch and then it swings open. I thought they must be hiding in the room above the dining room so I hopped out of bed and rushed on to the landing and all the doors on there were closed. I opened the storage room as we called it and turned on the light and there was no one in there, just obviously storage. It was just freezing and there was a slight smell of stale pee, like when the toilet hasn't been flushed in the men's toilet in work.

I went back to bed and I dreamt there was someone in the room. I could feel them by the side of my pillow, just crouched there, but I couldn't see anyone because of the dark. It was one of those awful dreams where you want to wake up but you can't. It felt like there was a pressure on my chest and I wanted to shout out but I couldn't.

I woke up around ten, which was late for me. I had a weird taste, a smell on me, it reminded me of when I was little and my nan would spit on her hanky and wipe my face. That sickly spit smell. I made the bed and I remember looking at it and thinking that it used to be my and Dai's bed, and how had everything gone wrong so quickly. I went downstairs, showered, made a cuppa and headed back up to get changed. As I started up the stairs I could smell that perfume, that sickly lavender and rose smell; on the landing the storage room door was open and when I went in the bedroom I screamed. I was so shocked. What was happening to me? The sheets for the bed which I know for certain I had made were balled up in the corner of the room. The bed was bare. The perfume was so incredibly strong that I ran and opened the bedroom window. I looked at the room and I just cried. I was going mad.

Dai: Anne called me, she was hysterical. She wasn't making much sense, just sobbing and I could hardly understand her. I was so worried that she had done something stupid like try and kill herself. I had visions of her slitting her wrists or taking pills. She had not been herself. She kept saying, "I'm sorry, I'm sorry."

I drove home and as soon as I got there she gave me a crushing hug. She was terrified, she didn't want to let go of me. She was like a child. My wife had always been so strong, and to see her like the way she had been was heartbreaking. I asked her what was happening and she just sobbed and sobbed and, finally, she said, "There's something in the house, Dai, there's something in the house."

Voices

Our very existence refuses your laws and your science, your religions and your philosophies.
BE Scully

It is not uncommon for one experiencing such activity to think they are becoming demented. Anne felt as if she no longer had control over her emotional and mental well-being. She would go on to explain that she felt as if she had been poisoned, that an unseen whisperer was planting seeds in her mind to break her resolve, to turn all she loved against her.

I had experienced the same level of intensity in the breakdown of a once loving relationship. All the doubts, insecurities and sadness of my past rushed back like a crashing wave upon the shore. How could something so special as a loving bond be shattered into a thousand pieces so rapidly? The entity was feeding off the negative energy that the breakdown was spawning. It was manifesting in a different way to which it had with me at the turn of the twenty-first century. This was less subtle. Had the phenomena been starved for so long that it was struggling to take purchase, or was it just using different tactics for different people? Horses for courses, so to speak.

Why were our perceptions different? Was it based on our own past experiences, the material that shapes our personality, which forms the person we are, or was it based on our emotional and mental tolerance? Were some people vulnerable and therefore easier to leech from, while others offered a more solid emotional defence forcing the entity to react accordingly with a more sustained and prolific attack?

Some could argue that all the events to this point are merely a mixture of misidentified occurrences, suggestion and a flawed mental state. Yet over a thirty-year period I have had six residents of that house, myself included, admit that something terrible happened within those four walls as well as the next-door neighbours' in 2003 (*A most haunted house*). Why would people decades and backgrounds apart consummate such a detailed hoax or even perceive rational events to be something more?

My work to bring as much detail to the testimony was paying dividends. I found the smell of lavender and rose particularly interesting as it was a very common fragrance used in Victorian Britain. So common that it could be made at home. Was the pungent smell the concoction from another time? Was this another clue to connect to the turn of the twentieth century? Was the entity using the events from a century previous to infect the present? What was it drawing upon that nourished this new terror? What had happened in the past that was so terrible it could mutilate the present in such a foul way. Could it be that my theory of an unnameable obscure power dwelling inside the house was incorrect, and that people that had committed great atrocities were juxtaposed into an altogether different layer of time, their ghosts and spirits lingering like the smell of decay? Had we been dealing with an ancient biblical creation such as a demon fuelled by the fires of hatred for all of God's archetypes? My instinct based on my own experience intimated that, whatever this thing was, it was not from our realm of understanding.

Hauntings take on many forms with occasional symptoms to the prolonged but never had I experienced a case that was taking on so many facets, many unique to the studies I had conducted. As disturbing as the account had been to date there were a great many terrifying and surreal aspects of the testimony yet to come. Events that could not be simply dismissed as misidentification or those which manifested from a paranoid mind.

Dai: It was a relief to get home. Anne was in such a state. She refused to go upstairs. She was convinced that someone was in the house, that someone was trying to split us up. I checked the house and I found nothing. She asked me to check again, and with my leg, I didn't want to go back up but she begged, and after another thorough search, nothing. She was acting so strange. I came downstairs the second time and I think it's best Anne tell you this part as she might not want to. It's up to her if she feels it relevant to the case.

Anne: So much of that morning was a blur. I was terrified I was losing my mind, I thought Dai was having an affair with my mum and I thought that there was a ghost in the house. I was all over the place. Did Dai tell you what I did? I'm so embarrassed and I feel very strange telling you this, but when Dai came down the stairs I had undressed and I was naked. I just felt compelled to take off my clothes. Dai was shocked. He said, was I OK, and all I could ask him was – did he still find me attractive, did he still want me? I was offering myself to him.

Dai: I told her she was beautiful and I loved her and we would get through this, but she kept grabbing me, telling me to touch her, prove that I loved her. I was hobbling around with my foot as she screamed why didn't I want her. I settled her down and I wrapped her in a towel and sat her on the settee, and I just held her and she cried. She said she was ugly and a bad person, and that I didn't deserve to be with her. It was not like her; in a week she had changed. I didn't know her anymore. it was a shock to see her like that, but I still loved her, the old Anne. I selfishly hoped there was a cure for this, you know, so things would get better and life would go back to normal.

Once she settled down, I called her mum and explained I was back in the house and that Anne wasn't feeling herself. She said she would come over and if I could pack a few of her things that she would take her back to hers for a bit. Just to take her out of the environment. A change is as good as a rest. I agreed. I was thinking, what if she doesn't get better? What if she had to go to a hospital? What if she never goes back to her old self? I felt very selfish for thinking like that.

Anne: I remember Mum coming over and I just sobbed and sobbed and told her how stupid I had been. And she just hugged me and said everything would be OK, and to just come back home, as in her house, for a break where she could look after me for a few days. She dressed me and I told her there was something in the house and she said not to overthink things; that I was just tired and stressed and I would be OK in a few days.

Dai: Anne and her mum left, and I was left alone in the house. I said I would call later to see if she felt any better. I honestly felt like a stranger in my own home. It didn't feel right without Anne. My brother rang and asked if I was OK and could he pop over, but I said I just wanted to get back to normal. I made some food and put on the TV.

I must have fallen asleep as when I woke it was dark outside, the TV was on. I thought, drat, I haven't called Anne. It was around eleven. I rang Anne's mum and she answered and said Anne had been asleep for pretty much the whole day, but in the morning she would give me an update. I thanked her for everything and sat back down and thought I would make some food. I must have been asleep for around six or seven hours and I had no idea how I would sleep that night.

I was in the kitchen making a sandwich when the radio went on behind me. I jumped out of my skin. It was playing a song, loudly. I can't remember what song it was as I turned it off sharpish. I turned back to making my supper when, from behind me, from the radio I can hear a whispering. It was like we heard before but clearer. I just stared at the radio and can hear a faint whispering. I listened and it sounded like a little child, girl or boy I could not tell, but it was whispering something. I was cautious not to put my head too close after last time but I could hear this child's voice, British I would say, but not loud enough. I could detect an accent repeating the same thing repeatedly: *"Go get the ax, there's a flea in Lizzie's ear, for a boy's best friend is his mother..."*

I did something I hope you are glad about. I didn't panic, I didn't throw out the radio. I went and grabbed the pen and paper, and I sat there just listening and trying to make sense of the words. The voice would get faint and drift out, and then come back clearer. The radio was off but I could still hear it. Now I remember many a time when I was younger that on the FM band you could pick up the police, taxies and even military now and again, so I thought was I picking up a baby monitor or another radio, TV perhaps?

This is what I wrote down that night.

Who cut the sleeves, out of dear old daddy's vest, and dug up Fido's bones to build the sewer?

I fell from a window, A second-story window, I caught my eyebrow on the window-sill.

Go get the ax there's a flea in Lizzie's ear, for a boy's best friend is his mother…

Note: The song Dai claims to have heard is called *Go Get the Ax* and was a popular song at the turn of the twentieth century. Research shows that it may have been a campfire song in the United States which was popularised between 1890 and 1935. Other theories are that it was a popular vaudeville song that may have originated in Britain during the late nineteenth century. How it connects to the house is still currently being researched.

Here are the complete lyrics of the song *Go Get the Ax*:

Peepin' through the knothole
Of grandpa's wooden leg,
Who'll wind the clock when I'm gone?
Go get the ax
There's a flea in Lizzie's ear,
For a boy's best friend is his mother.

Peepin' through the knothole
Of grandpa's wooden leg,
Why do they build the shore so near the ocean?
Who cut the sleeves
Out of dear old daddy's vest,
And dug up Fido's bones to build the sewer?

A horsey stood around,
With his feet upon the ground,
Oh, who will wind the clock when I'm gone?
Go get the ax,
There's a fly on Lizzie's ear,
But a boy's best friend is his mother.

I fell from a window,
A second-story window,
I caught my eyebrow on the window-sill.
The cellar is behind the door,
Mary's room is behind the ax,
But a boy's best friend is his mother.

Dai: People might think this strange, but to me, it made sense as I tried talking to the radio. I know it sounds daft, but you never know do you? Maybe the radio was receiving and transmitting so I was asking who was there, things like that. Could they hear me? Were they in Haverfordwest? All I heard was the same song, just bits of it for about fifteen minutes and then it faded out and nothing. I waited for it to come back. I sat perched on a stool in the kitchen just waiting for the radio to come back on.

Talking to you makes me feel like Anne and I were completely nuts, but still at this stage of living at the house we had not put all the pieces of the puzzle together. Both of us have had our own experiences, and I had tried to rationalise mine and Anne had just collapsed under the pressure.

I sat there for hours with a pen and paper just waiting. I had this idea that if the voices came back I would just press record and see if I could record it, and if that didn't work I would buy a tape recorder in the morning or borrow my brother's, who had one for his Spectrum Computer. I'm not sure what I was expecting to prove by recording it. Did I think it was something paranormal? Deep down maybe, but I was just looking for rational explanations so I could just get our life back to normal. I'm not an educated man by any stretch but I know what I know and I just wanted to start to make sense of all this. It was affecting Anne terribly and I had seen things like the shadow in the garden, felt the cold draughts and felt like someone was watching me when I lay down to sleep.

Nothing happened with the radio again that night and, around three, I made my bed up on the settee and lay there thinking about Anne, the house, what I had heard, just everything. I was lying in the dark. There was a little bit of street light coming in behind the blinds and I was staring into the room, and I thought I saw something moving in the shadows by the kitchen door. I couldn't be sure but it seemed as if something very tall – like exceptionally tall – was pacing back and forth. You have to remember that I was taking medication for my foot and I was all over the place with stress so I would not trust my judgement that night. I started to sit up and I peered into the dark when the phone rang. I jumped out of my skin, very horror movie I know, but trust me it's a lot scarier living it than seeing it on a screen.

I thought, who the hell is this now, at this time of night. Had the phone actually been ringing in the night and had Anne heard it? Maybe I had slept through it, maybe she had been right. I calmed down and thought, it's Anne, she's slept all day and now she has just woken up and panicked and she's calling me to say she's OK.

I picked up the phone and the reception was awful; it was crackling. I could hear someone breathing on the other end. I said, "Hello," and still just breathing. I thought, who the hell is playing silly buggers with us; we had been through enough as it was. I reasoned that maybe one of Anne's customers was drunk and messing around, I didn't know. I said hello again and still just the breathing and the crackling, so I said I was going and to piss off when I heard a voice, a man's, deep, very deep voice say: "Who cut the sleeves, Out of dear old daddy's vest."

I was so confused, I asked, "Who is this? What do you want?" I looked out of the blinds half expecting to see someone there. I didn't know if this was a joke or I had taken too many meds. I listened to that breathing and the crackling. It was hypnotic. I asked again who it was and the phone clicked and then the dial tone.

I was sat in the armchair all alone in the middle of the night, sat in the dark and I had heard voices on the radio and now on the phone, and to this day it raises the hairs on my arms not because of the voices but when I looked up and towards the kitchen I saw a tall dark figure, blacker than the shadows, make its way towards the stairs. And I sat there holding my breath and listened to the stairs creak as if someone was slowly taking each step at a time.

I had no idea at the time what it was. It was big and I was terrified. For as long as I live I will never be able to undo seeing that huge, I mean it had to be seven feet, figure walk across the room and I hear it walk up the stairs. I have no idea where it was going or what it was doing.

Did I chase after it; did I turn on the lights and investigate? No. I went back to my bed on the settee and I pulled the duvet over my head. Like a little boy, I just wanted to see the daylight again. I just wanted the night to be over. I heard many creaks and taps that night from upstairs. I don't know if it had anything to do with what I had seen but there was something up there. I was too scared to move and I held the duvet tight for I was scared I would hear it coming back down the stairs and pull the duvet off me. I was shivering and afraid, I'm not ashamed to admit that. Why didn't I run away, why did I stay? It was my home, Anne's home too, our home and as scared as I was, by leaving it then that would admit that this was real. I just wanted this all to go away.

I waited for morning and only one thing was going through my mind: *Who cut the sleeves, Out of dear old daddy's vest.*

Touched

I believe in everything until it's disproved. So, I believe in fairies, the myths, and dragons. It all exists. Even if it's in your mind, who's to say that dreams and nightmares aren't as real as the here and now.
John Lennon

I was intrigued by Dai's account of voices through the radio and the phone. Such things are not uncommon in today's paranormal landscape with EVP (*Electronic Voice Phenomena*) an integral part of any investigation. Investigators use recording equipment to record their conversations with unseen entities that may be present at the location and then play back to see if the device has captured a reply.

I once attended a private investigation at a house in Hakin, Pembrokeshire where a family claimed they were experiencing strange and worrying activity around their toddler. There were several investigators invited, attending from various fields and backgrounds, and we all used diverse methods of inquiry. The parents had claimed they had heard strange noises and sounds emitting from the baby monitor. I set up the baby monitor in a custom-built 3mm-thick iron box along with a digital recorder to block out as much radio interference as possible and recorded what sounded like a very strange voice saying, *"Little ones will burn."*

Both Nikola Tesla and Thomas Edison gave the notion enough merit to the extent they created devices for communicating with the spirit world, and in Tesla's case, an altogether different plane of existence.

Tesla had this to say about his experience using his 'spirit' radio invention in 1901:

> *My first observations positively terrified me as there was present in them something mysterious, not to say supernatural, and I was alone in my laboratory at night.*

He then added in 1918:

> *The sounds I am listening to every night at first appear to be human voices conversing back and forth in a language I cannot understand. I find it difficult to imagine that I am actually hearing real voices from people not of this planet. There must be a more simple explanation that has so far eluded me.*

From 1979 to 1982, George Meek and Bill O'Neil developed a device they dubbed the *Spiricom* (*short for spirit communication*). The Spiricom was a set of 13 tone generators spanning the frequency range of the adult male voice. Recordings of the Spiricom in action still exist today, though nobody has been able to duplicate the results, to date. The Spiricom gave off a loud buzz when in operation, due to the frequency generators. The idea was to use the different frequency waves being generated as a carrier signal of the voice of any willing disembodied human who spoke from the other side of the grave.

There are so many examples and research into the phenomena that a dozen books would not do the subject justice.

Should Dai be honest in his testimonial then how could such an entity use modern man-made equipment to vocalise and communicate. A broad sweep of paranormal entities (alien, spirit, demon and dimensional, if in fact they are not one and the same) are said by many within the field to consist of energy that can be measured by electrical devices. Therefore, it stands to reason that they can manipulate electrical objects around us. They could try to get our attention by making lights flicker or even turn things on or off. What if they use the electricity that is wrapped around us, hidden in the walls and ceilings, to feed off to create the initial manifestation, to allow themselves to become established within our world so they can further feast off the negativity created? Or maybe in places that have no electricity, it simply uses the energy a person emits to take hold in that environment.

Who was the man Dai had heard on the telephone that night? Did the voice belong to the shadow seen emerging from the darkness? Was the towering and intimidating figure the now notorious Angry Man? A figure that is known for its violent and aggressive behaviour (*A most haunted house*). Was this how the entity wished to be perceived, as a sizeable and oppressive presence? A reader cannot truly fathom the fear induced by such close proximity to the Angry Man. It is something utterly terrifying and abysmal that I hope you never have to experience.

Anne: Time at Mum's did me the world of good. After a day and a good night sleep I woke up and felt like I had woken from a terrible dream. I could not work out what was real and what was part of the nightmare. I was confused. It is like when you have drunk too much the night before, and the next day you wake up and you have no idea where you are or how you got there.

Mum was up and we sat and talked. I asked her what had been happening and she asked how much did I remember. I remembered thinking Dai had been having an affair and just melting down. Mum told me everything. It was embarrassing and I felt so awful. I was ashamed of how I treated Dai and my mum. I asked Mum if I was ill or something, did I need to see a doctor and she replied that I should have another day or two at hers and see how I felt. I rang Dai and he sounded so tired. I apologised so much to him, and said I didn't know what had come over me. He said it was OK and that to have a few days at Mum's while he caught up on some sleep, and we could talk when we saw each other again and start over. He was amazing, he so understood, but his voice sounded weird. He said he was tired, stressed and his foot was hurting.

I felt so guilty. I told him I loved him so much and that I would go and get help if that was needed to get me back to normal. I didn't talk to him about the bedroom and the smell as I really needed him to think I was better, and to be honest I doubted myself so much. Ghosts don't exist, do they? You can't go around telling everyone a ghost is making a mess and wearing horrible perfume. Now I can talk to you about it openly with complete confidence because if people don't believe me then I'm happy for them as that means they haven't had to experience what we did. I don't know how it all worked but I know it was real. It's like a plane; I know it can fly but I don't understand how.

Dai: Anne rang me the next morning, and bless her she was so sorry. I missed her so much and I wanted us back together. I wasn't angry with her, I just didn't understand what was going on. I started to feel low; I was putting on weight and I was brooding a lot. I didn't mention my night alone in the house to her because I didn't know if she was actually ill in the head or not yet. I didn't want to upset her or fuel her paranoia. I remember asking for a few days to get some sleep and tidy up the house; but really, I wanted to find out more about what was happening in the damn house.

It was about then I got the tape recorder and hobbled down to the library on Dew Street and started investigating. I didn't really know where to start. I told a lady who worked there that I was trying to find out a bit of history of where I lived and she was eager to help. I got lots of stuff of Haverfordwest in general, some parish records, but nothing that was useful. I even showed her part of the song I had written down and she said she had never heard of it. I was not an investigator. I probably read one book a year while on holiday and that was normally something to do with sport. There was no Internet back then so it was tough going.

Did I think it was something paranormal? Even then I was

thinking hallucinations, that the hospital had given me the wrong drugs for my foot. My theory of gas seeping up through the floor... I was not ready to admit, despite everything, that this was anything unexplainable. I hoped to find some records of people who had similar experiences in the same house, same street or even same town. I read through the *Western Telegraph* archives and found nothing; though, I did read a bit about the UFO sightings in the late 70s and thought maybe was it something to do with that.

How did I think that? Well, I never believed it was aliens; I always thought it was all to do with the RAF (Royal Air Force) and the Yanks at their airbase. They were building submarine tracking bases, early warning radars and all kinds of stuff to track the Russians. It was regular to see fighters and Sea Kings flying around the county. I always thought, what if there had been a chemical spill or the submarine base was emitting a signal that was messing with people's heads and they were then seeing UFOs and giant spacemen? I just thought maybe that was what was happening to us too. I couldn't tell you how or why, but as I keep saying at this stage I was not ready to accept that these were ghosts or whatever you think it is.

Anne: While I was at my mother's I pretty much became myself again. I missed Dai terribly and I felt I was ready to come home. We spoke every night on the phone and we planned a night out for a pint and food like old times. The pub owner was right; I needed a bit of time and space to sort my head out. I remember vividly thinking to myself, don't mention the weird spooky stuff, Dai is at the house and everything is OK. It was in my head and just forget it now. It wasn't till later I found out that Dai had witnessed the arrival of the Angry Man as it was called in *A most haunted house*.

Dai: I think I was alone for around three nights in total, with Anne at her mum's. I had the tape recorder ready and I also bought a Polaroid instant camera. I had the radio on and made sure the phone volume was up, and nothing happened. Not a tap, not a sound, nothing. I was so nervous; I was on edge just waiting for something to happen and nothing did. Every time the phone went in the day I would jump out of my skin, but it was just a normal phone call from Anne or my family. Nothing happened at all and Anne came home and it was good to have her home. I thought this could be it, the start of a normal life again. I needed to shake off this sadness I was feeling all the time. I did make sure, however, that I hid the camera and tape recorder as I didn't want to make her think something was going on.

Anne: It was great to be home. The house was nice and tidy, and Dai gave me a big hug and a big kiss. There was no smell of that perfume, nothing, just as it was before. We were intimate on the settee and I knew we were OK. We had missed each other so much. A few days later I was back in work and Dai was at home with his foot up in front of the TV, recovering.

Dai: It all went very quiet. I slept downstairs and nothing happened. I hoped it was over. Every day I got more and more depressed. I hated being alone in the house even though nothing was happening. I used to think about my mum dying or what would happen when I died. I was thinking about death a lot and sex too. I would brood that I would get too fat and Anne would leave me, and I would not be able to find anyone else. I started to feel very alone and miserable so just started drinking a few cans in the day, you know, to buck me up, give me some pep as my uncle would say when people were down. I hoped whatever I thought was happening was over. It is never over at that house, is it? It's still happening now I bet.

Anne: Life was good for a bit. Dai seemed to be on the mend and it was good in work and Jimmy the patron apologised and I said sorry back and Mum was popping over more in the week to help me and Dai, and it was great.

I got home one night and I was shattered. It was around

August Bank Holiday. I will check my journal but it was mid to late August 1990 when things started up again. I went straight to bed and Dai was out of it, fast asleep, still on the couch. I think this was the last night he slept down there. I get into bed and we had plans coming up; and as tired as I was, I was excited. You know when you can't switch off and you can't sleep? I'm lying there when I feel a draught on my face. I knew the window was closed so I turned on my side and pulled the duvet up to my face.

My heart started to beat so hard and fast when I thought I felt something sit by the side of the bed. Right by me. I didn't want to reach over and turn on the lamp as I thought something would grab me and I heard a woman whisper something in my ear and I screamed. It was so real. I felt breath on my ear and I could smell tea breath.

I grabbed for the light and I knocked it over and got tangled up in the duvet. I was petrified. I imagined someone there in the dark, someone that would grab my arm or pull my hair. I screamed for Dai.

Dai: Anne's screaming woke me up. I was so disorientated and thought, not now, not again. I couldn't handle much more of this. I managed to get up there and turn on the light in the bedroom and Anne was lying on the floor with a pillow over her face and I could hear her screaming into it.

I grabbed her and she lashed out at me. I told her to calm down, that it was me, and she peered from behind the pillow. She was frightened half to death. I asked her what was wrong and she said that a woman was in the room and had sat on the bed and spoken to her.

Anne: Dai said the strangest thing, it totally took me back. He asked, *"What did she say?"*

Dai: I don't know really, well, I wanted to know if the voice had sung that song to her. Anne said she wasn't sure what it said, a lot of gibberish and nonsense which made me feel uneasy. I told her maybe it was a dream and she said she had not even been asleep. She was worried that she was having an episode again, but I calmed her and reassured her that it was all OK, and I would sleep back upstairs again. She must have asked a million times what was going on and I didn't tell her, as what good would it do? We had no proof of anything and what would we do – leave our home because of shadows and dodgy electrics?

Anne: This is a classic case of bad communication between couples. He knew things from the first weekend and things with the radio and the tall figure, and I knew that the house was wrong, but we were trying to protect each other and not talk about it. I thought I was going mad and Dai was convinced there was a rational explanation. If only we had spoken about it sooner.

I was petrified that night but I gave in and said that I must have been dreaming, and Dai looked worried. I thought if he thinks I'm on the turn again, losing my mind, he will break up with me after everything I put him through. I was so confused, so conflicted. I just wanted to scream, "We need to leave!"

Dai: I just remember being so low, so fed up. I couldn't talk to Anne because she was so mentally fragile. Well that's what I convinced myself. And if I started to talk about the house being haunted and all this mad stuff happening then I would set her going again. The next few nights changed all of that.

Anne: The next night Dai slept in bed with me. His foot was on the mend and he was off his meds, but he had started drinking in the day. Not too much but enough that as soon as he got into bed, he would be out like a light and start snoring. He had put on weight, but then he was less active and stuck at home so I was easy on him.

I was lying there and I'm thinking, what if there really is something here, ghosts, spirits, whatever it is, and we are lying here in the dark and they are just watching us. Who knows what goes on in our homes while we are asleep? How many of us wake in the night to a bang or a thump and just think something has fallen and we forget about it. We spend so much time on keeping people out with alarms and locks, but what if there is already something inside your house. Just watching you sleep, watching you pee, shower, make love. I think we look at ghosts and spirits as harmless, but they are not; they are not at all.

I managed to drop off, that weird slumber where you are half-awake but have weird dreamy thoughts, when something snapped me out of it. I just felt there was something in the room. I was too scared to look. When I was a little girl I always thought if I can't see it then it can't hurt me. I could feel something in the room; it felt like it was creeping towards me. Dai was snoring heavily and I just wanted to wake him up. I felt the air change in the room. It got colder and I could smell a hint of lavender and rose. With the duvet over my head and my eyes closed as tight as I could, I just said in my head this song we used to sing in school at the end of each day, and in my head over and over I said, *"If I should die before I wake."* I'm not religious, I only went to church for weddings. I don't know why I felt the need to sing this.

I was balled up under the duvet like a foetus, and between Dai's snoring I could hear something moving around. The smell got stronger, lavender and rose. Over and over I sang in my head, *"If I should die before I wake. If I should die before I wake. If I should die before I wake."*

The pressure in the room was so intense, my knees were up to my chest and my arms wrapped around them and my chin tucked deep into my chest. I just imagined the old woman with flypaper skin just stood by the bed, reaching down to me. I felt like I was five again. Things like this are not supposed to be real.

I woke up and Dai was already up and I could hear him down in the kitchen, and I thought I must have been dreaming; it had felt so real. I was so confused by what was real and what was a dream that I struggled to tell the difference. I woke up in a ball under the duvet but the one thing that made me sick, made me so worried, was my mouth and face smelt and tasted of granny spit.

Dai: Anne was quiet the next morning. I found no joy in life and started on the cans early. One way or another, depending on your opinion, that night was the last night there were doubts. What happened next, I can't fully understand to this day. This is the part of our experience that really put us off telling other people, because some will think us mad, others fraudsters, some mentally ill. Every know-it-all sceptic debunker that hides behind words and science that has never experienced anything like this will laugh and discredit when they have eff-all knowledge of anything. It's people like them that make it so hard to open up and try and make sense of it all. It is people like them who laugh at it without even trying to understand. How many people out there are too scared to talk and get help because of idiots that think they know it all when in fact they know nothing? It makes me so angry. What Anne and I went through no person should have to go through. We had no one to turn to; we would have been laughed out of town.

If people want to know why I'm doing this, why I'm talking to Gavin, why I'm allowing him to write this book, it is so that people can open up, open up and get it off your chest. You, the ones living through this, you are not the ones to blame. The last few weeks have been the greatest therapy I could have asked for. It's been a hard time bringing all of it up but it has helped to talk about it. I have not been judged or laughed at, I feel like someone cares. Whatever is behind all of this at least now we are not living some little secret that we should be ashamed of talking about because some people can't deal with it. I'm sorry, I just get so frustrated, and thirty years we have carried this as if we were the ones in the wrong.

Anne: Yeah, that was the night before the night. This is so hard to talk about.

Dai: I had been having a few cans in the day; just to cheer me up but to be honest I was beyond low. I was convinced that my mum was going to die and Anne would leave me, and I started sleeping in the day too.

Anne: I went to work that day and I couldn't get that taste of granny spit out of my mouth. I had brushed my teeth twice. It made me sick.

Dai: I woke up around four in the afternoon and went downstairs and turned the TV on, so when Anne came home it was as if everything was normal. Men back then were not supposed to be depressed.

Anne: I got home and I was shattered, I was so tired. That taste had gone and I enjoyed my dinner; the taste had put me off eating all day. Dai was quiet and he said he was just tired. He said he was looking forward to going back to work. He had put on so much weight that it wasn't helping his leg much. He didn't talk about sport or much at all.

Dai: I got so fat but I can't remember eating more; just drinking and no exercise, I guess? We were both acting so strange at that time. It would have been easy for someone to have locked us up and thrown away the key.

Anne: I had a shower and headed up to bed early that night as I needed a good night's sleep. I made myself not think of the house and the weird stuff as I thought maybe I was imagining too much, looking for things that weren't there. And I thought if I don't think of it, it won't happen. Like I was a magnet for it.

Dai: I stayed up, *Match of the Day* [*football TV show*] was on, and I didn't feel tired at all after my five or six hours' sleep in the day.

Anne: I fell asleep quickly and had another awful dream. I have been worried about this part all week since we last spoke. I even thought not to tell you. It is awful. I know you are here to help us understand, but this is truly vile. I close my eyes even to this day and it's like I am in that room.

In my dream, a nightmare I guess, I was back in the house but again back as it was. I was lying in the bedroom. The bed was where it is now. It was daytime, a light was coming in from the window but the glass was all cracked and dirty and I couldn't see anything out there.

I couldn't move. It was like when you have sleep paralysis, it feels so very real. I could feel how cold it was in there and I could smell boiled onions or something like it. The bedroom is the same shape as it is now, a window in the same place, but the walls are grey and the paint is peeling off. There are dirty, yellow linen curtains which are covered in mould hanging over the windowsill. I could see a wooden dresser against the wall by the door. There are candles on it. I can't see any pictures or anything else.

The door opens and the old woman with flypaper skin is stood there in her brown dress. I'm scared she will shout at me. She stares at me and smiles. Her teeth were black. She walked towards the bed and she is singing this song that made no sense. I watched her walk to my side of the bed and she looked down at me and licked her lips; she didn't stop singing that strange song. She started to undress and took off her brown dress and she had on a one-piece underwear garment, a very old-fashioned looking thing, which is dirty and stained. The knickers bit is stained with pee.

(Anne requests a break as she begins crying; it takes several minutes for her to compose herself.)

Anne: Thank you, well, this is so wrong, first the animals and now this. I dread to think what people will say. The old woman pulls down her shoulder straps and pulls down her top exposing these saggy old boobs. Her neck is just hanging skin like a turkey and her skin, a yellow brown, is covered in veins and liver spots. She is stinking of lavender and rose too. I can't move, I can't wake up; I just wanted this to stop.

She climbs on top of me. She never stops singing that song. I look towards the door, just praying someone will run in. I pray it will be Dai to rescue me from this; and in the door, there are two children. Not very tall at all, the boy in grey shorts and a grey jacket, the girl in a faded grey dress, her hair long and dirty down to her elbows. I wanted to scream. They were both singing this awful song in time with the old woman. Neither child had any facial features apart from a mouth. It was if there was a blur covering their faces. I wanted them to help me, to make this stop.

The old woman dangled her breasts across my face and she laughed and started rocking above me. She leant over and started to kiss me, lick me, that stinking smell of granny spit, tea and rotten teeth. I felt her tongue in my mouth and I thought I was going to suffocate. I couldn't wake up! Even now I remember that vile taste and smell of granny spit.

Dai: I was watching TV when I heard this strange howling sound from upstairs. This strange muffled noise almost like an animal in pain. I turned down the TV and it was coming from above me, from the bedroom. I could hear the bed creaking too. I thought, what was going on up there, and headed up.

Anne: It seemed to last forever. It was like she was having sex with me, as a woman would with a man. She threw her head back like she was close to, you know, orgasm? It was horrific. She and the children just sang and sang and I couldn't stop it. It was like I was being raped.

Dai: I got into the room and turned on the light. What I saw I cannot comprehend, I can't undo from my mind. Anne was lying in the bed, the duvet on the floor; the room smelt of perfume and on Anne, over Anne was a dark shadowy shape. Not a just shadow, but a shape, shadowy and see-through and underneath Anne's face was contorted. She was making these awful sounds. I had never seen anything so terrifying like this in my life.

I screamed at it and grabbed Anne's hand. The thing

disappeared like smoke and Anne woke up. She looked at me for a second and began screaming. It took a long time that night to make her stop. We knew now that this was real. We knew now that we were not alone in this house and something terrible was living here with us.

Defiance

What I am afraid of is the first thing I was ever aware of being afraid of and what I have told my daughter countless times she need not fear: being alone in the dark. It is a small prison of emotion from which there is no escape. It is also, in its own way, a shattering revelation.
SC Gwynne

Spectrophilia, sex with spirits and/or paranormal entities, is a subject I am very familiar with after documenting the Pembroke Dock paranormal sexual abuse case in my second book, *Ghost sex: The Violation*. For those not familiar with the controversial and challenging testimony, a middle-aged woman residing in Pembroke Dock, West Wales claimed to have been the victim of paranormal sexual abuse for decades by not one but two very different paranormal phenomena.

It was a deeply demanding interview and investigation that stretched my comprehension of the paranormal to the furthest reaches. It was described as harrowing and dehumanising. It was an ordeal an ordinary woman was forced to endure not just at her home but wherever she went. Upon publication, a great many people came forward with their own graphic and brutal accounts of paranormal sexual abuse. I felt terribly ill-equipped to deal with so much anger, grief and concern over a subject I stumbled upon while investigating a less traumatic field of paranormal study, imaginary friends.

I was assisted, with great appreciation on my part, by a psychologist called AS Hawking, who helped me discern the psychological issues and events that may cause a subject to believe they are the target of paranormal abuse, harassment and sexual misuse and corruption. Were these people truly powerless at the whim of an unseen force or was it merely a malfunction in one's psychology? *Ghost sex: The Violation* would go to great lengths in the rational explanations that could make a person believe these unwanted intrusions were a very real occurrence, explanations that would contradict Anne's claim.

Anne was still mentally scarred by the events of that house. How had her dream manifested into a reality that Dai had witnessed? How did her inward violation become an actual assault? If what he had seen was real, then was the entity feeding off her? Was it creating an environment within her mind to cause the uttermost anxiety, helplessness and fear to leech from; or again, had disturbing actions from the past layered themselves on to their present?

Was the grotesque old woman described an embodiment of the old hag syndrome? The night hag or old hag is a generic name for a fantastical creature from the folklore of various peoples which is used to explain the phenomenon of sleep paralysis. A common description is that a person feels a presence of a supernatural malevolent being which immobilises the person as if sitting on his or her chest. Is there a part of our brain that mobilises the imagery of this old hag when one is under huge amounts of pressure? Anne believed it to be real and corroborated by Dai's perception of the event. Anne is still deeply affected by the vision of an old haggard woman forcefully sexually abusing her. Imagine before you sleep tonight that image, that feeling of helplessness, the violation and then contemplate how Anne must feel.

Dai's depression and Anne's continued anxiety is common within this field of research to the extent that I published an article on The Paranormal Chronicles website asking, "DEPRESSION: Has a paranormal ENTITY latched onto you???" The article was read by thousands across the world, many of whom all had their own paranormal events which deeply dulled their shine and love of life. Hundreds of people all claimed that until strange inexplicable occurrences began, they had been happy with their circumstances, were not prone to depression, had valued and appreciated the gift of life; but soon feelings of positivity dwindled into those of melancholy and dispiritedness.

As the paranormal continues to be a subject that is not given enough merit by the scientific community, how are we ever able to help these people who believe such terrible things are happening to them? Should we simply deem everyone mentally ill and dose them up on pharmaceuticals and numb them to an existence of misery. Can everyone simply assume that the days we feel low are just because of physical changes to the brain, neurotransmitters and hormones, and depression merely a condition of life that we should just accept? Should we not take seriously the claims of those who feel a paranormal entity has taken hold of them, is feeding upon their negativity? How many people have lost their resolve and ended their suffering because no one was there to try and understand?

It is a challenging theory that may do more harm than good if people will not consult professional guidance. Yet again, what if that professional help is not the adequate countermeasure for a real paranormal threat if such things were to exist? Can we confidently knock such notions, content in our understanding of the universe, when once before we were equally confident in our belief the world was flat and the sun rotated around the Earth?

Dai and Anne have harboured their experience as an obscure secret for decades, worried that they will be labelled as frauds or mentally ill. It is not until you spend many hours with these people that you see them as just that, people. People like you who want a happy life, to work, to love, to nurture a family. It is so sad that so many do not have the support they need to make sense of such an experience. Ask yourself, how confident would you be to go to your doctor and say you think you are being haunted?

Sadly, for Dai and Anne, this was not the end, far from it. The intensity of the events that were to come are as astonishing as they are hideous.

Dai: Anne would not stop screaming and crying. She howled that she had been raped and that she was losing her mind. I told her she wasn't, I had seen it, it was real. She stopped and stared at me and asked, "What?" I told her I had seen the figure, the shadow lying on her, and she just started laughing. I was so unnerved by it all. I was worried that she had been, you know, possessed. What if it wasn't my Mrs in there anymore?

Anne: It was so vivid, so real and so awful. I think I was in shock as I can't remember much other than crying and sobbing. I remember running downstairs and brushing my teeth, just trying to get rid of the taste and smell of granny spit. I felt like everything I knew of the world was turned upside down when Dai told me he believed me, he said he had seen something. I thought for a moment, what if he is drugging me up, making me go mad; but he looked as scared and as shocked as I was.

Dai: She calmed down and it was around three in the morning and I said put on your dressing gown and let's go. I persuaded her to get into the car and we drove and parked up in Tesco car park [*supermarket*]. We just needed to be away from the house.

Anne: We sat in the car at Tesco in the middle of the night. I was shaking. I still had that awful taste in my mouth. I thought, what if the police come? What do we say? We fled our house because an old lady raped me in my dream but it's OK, officer, because my husband saw her do it... but it wasn't an old lady just a black blob. It was like we had lost our minds. Was there something in the water? In the air? Was it just us? A million things fly through your mind but all I could think of was that old woman's disgusting old face and saggy tits. Every time I thought of it I would just sob. I had to leave the car to be sick.

Dai: I was shaking and scared. I didn't know what to do. I thought about driving to my mum's. But Anne said no, we had to make a story that made sense as they will think we were sick in the head. I said that in the morning I would book us into a hotel and we could regroup and try and make sense of this.

Anne: I asked Dai, did he know about this? He went quiet and I hit him so much. I feel awful but I must have screamed and slapped him a dozen times and he just took it.

Dai: My face was raw and I started to cry. I just couldn't take anymore and then she hugged me and said she was sorry. It was a terrible time.

Anne: He told me everything. He told me about the shadow in the garden, he told me about the radio and the phone and the huge shadow walking up the stairs. He told me about the song, and it felt like a cold knife gutted me because as he said the words, I remembered them as the song the old woman and the kids were singing, the same words that were whispered into my ear.

Dai: We sat in the car silent from then till around five. Around that time people started turning up for work so we drove for an hour or two. I had to go back to the house. Anne didn't want me too but I ran in and grabbed a few bags of clothes, toiletries, money, just stuff to last us a few days. It was worrying going back in the house. I expected to be set upon by shadows. Nothing happened and I got us booked in at the Mariners hotel in Haverfordwest.

Anne: I can't even remember getting to the hotel or checking in.

Dai: I ran Anne a bath and she sat in it crying for ages. I didn't have a plan other than we couldn't go back to the house. We needed to sell up and get out of there. I thought maybe we could stay with our family till the sale of the house went through. I was very angry but I was trying to keep calm. I felt how I would if a man was molesting Anne. There was nothing for me to unleash at so I used my energy into keeping Anne safe and as calm as I could.

Anne: I had a bath and just slept. I was exhausted. I woke up and Dai was sitting in a chair just staring at me. He was watching over me in case that thing, that shadow came back.

Dai: I told Anne my plan and she surprised me. She said that we weren't going to let this win. She reminded me that the old man had lived there for decades and he was OK; and I reminded her that he died a sad, lonely death from cancer that riddled his body. How did we know that the thing in the house was not to blame for that? I told her, maybe we could end up like that?

Anne: I didn't want to leave the house. I know I was terrified but what if we could oust it? I had read about and seen in films that you could get exorcists and mediums to come to the house and dispel the evil, the ghosts, demons, whatever it was.

Dai: It was hard to accept that this was paranormal but I couldn't explain what I had seen. We talked about the bones in the garden and the shadow creature, dog thing I saw, and was that when it all started? Anne said that maybe I had freed the animals' souls from their grave and that was them thanking me. The more we talked about souls and spirits, ghosts and demons, the more I thought I was living in some kind of nightmare. Where was Jeremy Beadle when you needed him?

Anne: We opened up and we talked about all of it, from the beginning to the night previous. I started to take control, I started to plan. Dai was nervous and said we should just sell up and go. How could we do that? It's not going to happen overnight, we would need a place to live and living in the spare room of our families would not be right. Plus we were OK for money but living in a hotel would make us broke in no time. So would trying to rent while taking on a mortgage too.

I had to shout at Dai to calm him down to listen. All he said was, "We got to leave there. We have to go." He had got off lightly as far as I was concerned. I was the one the thing was attached to. I said we would be smart and we would beat this thing. Stupid I know, but would you want to just give in? My family fights for what it believes in and what we love, and we had worked hard to buy that house. Why should we go when it can go? I guess that I was thinking of this thing as you would a rat or woodworm. I thought we have power over it, not the other way around.

My plan sounds daft but I said we would take shifts sleeping, we would sleep with the light on and we would watch each other. Dai could sleep in the day and I would at night. We would collect as much evidence as we could no matter what the risk and we would get help, whether it was professional, exorcists, mediums, the Pope, Rambo, I didn't care. We would put a crucifix in every room if we had to; we put a Bible by the bed and prayed every night. My fear and anger turned to the will to fight and to destroy this thing. I could feel it in my chest. I thought it was the right thing to do.

Dai: I was not sold on her plan at all. I thought she had been watching too much TV. I remember saying to her that we are just simple people, living an ordinary life. There may still be a rational explanation to all this, but either way, the house is making us ill and we are breaking down. Anne is very persuasive and said, "Please, let's fight this, let's get help, and find out what's happening there." I made her promise if another night like that night happened again though we would leave and never come back. I would burn that house to the ground before we lost each other.

Anne: I agreed. We were going to beat this thing.

Dai: How many people reading this are thinking, "What the hell, they went back?" They must think we are idiots.

Anne: We went back to the house the next day. I called into work and said I had sickness and diarrhoea, the sure-fire way to get a few days off, and the first thing I did was scrub that house from top to bottom. I washed the bedding, hoovered every inch of carpet, polished every surface. In my mind that was part of the fight. We were leaving our mark on the house; we were cleaning away the negativity, the ghosts. We had the music on and the TV, and I cooked us a nice Sunday dinner even though it was a Friday.

I had a journal which hadn't been filled in much that year but I started from that day. Here have a look. On Friday, 31st August 1990, I have written: "Back at home. Cleaned and made it our home again. Made a nice dinner. We will not lose our home or each other."

People can say how they can remember so much from all that time ago; but first you don't forget, as hard as you try, the things that happened then, and the journal helped me too. I honestly thought that this would be the change. How could I just let go of what happened with terrifying dreams and the shape on me; what could I do? Cry my whole life? Hide away? Go to the police? We Pembrokeshire Girls take control and we get on with it.

Dai: I thought she was mad, but as she said, what else were we to do? I still thought we should leave and take our chances out there.

Anne: That night, Dai slept and I stayed awake and nothing happened, apart from in the morning the storage room door was opened. I didn't hear it open; I just sat up in bed reading the Bible, a first for everything. I was scared, yes, but at the same time I had faith that we could beat this. I just thought a Bible would be a weapon, just having it made me feel safe. I'm not religious, not even now. I'm spiritually aware now. Whatever that thing was and wherever it came from, it would not be made by any God that is supposed to love us, give us free will and all that. We would learn this was something entirely different, nothing to do with the universe we live in. Mad, I know!

I closed the cupboard door as if nothing had happened and thought I will close that door a thousand times if I have to. We did that all week and the only thing that happened was the storage room door would be open each morning.

Dai: She told me about the cupboard door and I told her about how I had bought a Polaroid and a tape recorder. She said she would set the recorder up on the landing; it was only a thirty-minute cassette. It gives me goosebumps thinking about listening back to those recordings. The house is so quiet and you can hear me snoring and that is about it. Anne would get up and change the tape over so we would have at least an hour's worth. On one recording, you can hear the latch on the storage door clink and you can hear it swing open.

We don't have the tapes, I know, it's so stupid. We lost the photograph too of the thing in the bed that we took later. I would give a million pounds to have that box back. It got lost in the move; it was stupid to have lost it. Maybe someone out there has a shoebox of old tapes and Polaroids. If you have, just look at the headboard picture and get in touch with Gavin.

Anne: Yeah, skipping forward a bit, nothing was really happening. We recorded the storage door being unlatched in the night, and apart from a few cold spots, it was quiet. I can't remember any disgusting dreams for a while when Dai and I swapped shifts to sleep. Things weren't any easier, but they were manageable. Dai was signed off to go back to work in November, so we had two months to work this out.

I was in bed reading and Dai was on the landing taking random pictures, and he walked in and took a picture of the bedroom from the door. He was waiting for the print to pop out and he shook it, looked at it and his face was horrified. I asked him to show me, and he just looked so worried. I demanded he show me, and in the picture, you could see me in bed and just above my head, in the headboard, was a blob of light and in the blob of light, you could clearly see a face. It looked like the face of an old man in glasses. I leapt out of bed to look and I couldn't see anything. Dai took about a dozen more pictures and there was nothing in them. Dai was ready for us to leave, but I said we would be OK. It hadn't hurt us, just scared us.

To be safe that night I slept on the sofa and Dai sat up watching TV. I was scared. An old man's face was something new but we had to stay strong.

Dai: I'm not sure what to make of the picture; he looked like an old man's face in a pair of glasses. It wasn't a flat face though; the way it was angled it looked like he was peering down at Anne. You could see the shape of his nose and chin. White balding hair, gaunt and with black-rimmed old-fashioned glasses. I know there is that thing where you can see faces in clouds but I wish to God I could show you this picture: there was a man's head staring down at Anne. Like it was reading her book with her. Anne thinks she solved the mystery though.

Something else strange happened that night that was overshadowed by the picture and something I haven't really discussed, but Anne was asleep on the settee and I was keeping watch. I had the TV off as there was nothing on and I just had the light on in the kitchen, which was enough light so I could see, or to be honest, not be terrified of being sat there in the dark but not bright enough it would keep Anne awake. I nipped for a pee and just for a second from the corner of my eye I swore I saw a red glow coming from the mantelpiece and the shadow of something sat in front of it. I quickly turned on the main light and there was nothing there.

You must remember that there was so much going on that every noise and shadow was becoming something more. It could have been my eyes playing up having come from the light of the bathroom to the darker dining and living rooms. I just thought of Anne's dream of being sat there by the fire hurting animals. I wondered if I had seen a flashback of that. I'm not sure, it happened so quick and from the corner of my eye, so who knows in that house?

Anne: The day after that I had an idea and I called my friend in Milford, the one who knew the house, and I asked her to describe her ex-boyfriend's dad, and she said when she last saw him he had greying receding hair and glasses. I told her everything apart from the dreams and she didn't say I was mad.

She said that Harold [*not his real name*] who had lived there would not do her any harm. Even though she hardly knew him, she just had a sense that he was not like that. She didn't think he would have been responsible for the animal remains, and if there was something bad in the house then maybe he was looking after us.

I asked her to pop over and showed her the picture, and she said it looked like a very ill version of the Harold she knew. Maybe it had been him at the end of his life but she didn't think he would hurt us. I liked the idea that he was protecting us, but it also upset me that in spirit you still looked like how you had died. What if you had been badly burned or killed in a terrible accident? I have heard since that there is a ghost at Withybush Hospital of a man that is horribly burned that roams one of the wards.

My friend was very understanding and one of the few people I told. She said that hauntings were common and she knew a woman who might be able to help us and bless the house. She was very spiritual, and I felt so much better for telling her. I wish she was here to tell you herself about the picture and those few months, but she died in 2007. I miss her so much. She would have helped you so much with this, and she was a firm believer in the spiritual world and the supernatural. She said she could sense an unwelcoming presence in our home and that Rose, the medium spiritualist woman, would be able to help cleanse the house.

She told me Rose did not work for money, did not do shows or charge people and that you wouldn't find her in the *Yellow Pages*, but she would talk to her and arrange for her to come over. Apparently, she had met her at a spiritualist church a few years back. Rose was very well known within that circle, and apparently, even the proper Church had asked her to assist with a few hauntings.

Dai: Anne told me that a woman was going to come over and bless the house, but it wasn't going to be for a few weeks as the lady was away looking after a family member. To be honest, I didn't care if this woman had powers or could help; I just wanted it to stop. I asked, if her friend from Milford was such a big believer and knew more about it, then why was she not here staying with us, and Anne said she had three boys to look after.. I needed someone else to see and feel what we were witnessing, to make it real in my head.

It sounds almost like a catchphrase now but things were quiet in the house again. You said in *A most haunted house* that you felt like the house would recharge ready for its next attack. Well it was doing just that. Just recharging ready for the next round.

Anne: I was making dinner in the kitchen and Dai was watching TV. It was only a few days before we had booked this woman to come and see us. Her name was Rose. She's dead now. She was old back then, she had to be in her late seventies. Anyway, back to dinner. It was latish around eight and it's late September and it's dark outside. I've got the radio on and Dai is watching TV, when the light flickered in the kitchen, just a quick flicker. The temperature drops and from the corner of my eye I thought I saw a dark shadow, man sized – just barely visible – walk past me from the kitchen door leading to the garden. I spun around and the temperature just dropped, like freezing cold and the radio began clacking, this terrible high-pitched interference.

I went to turn off the radio and again from the corner of my eye saw this tall shadow in the living room. You couldn't look at it directly. Dai stands up quickly and the TV has gone to that static screen, all those black and white dots. The lights went off in the house and I screamed. I knew that shadow was in the house and I was too scared to move.

Dai: I was watching TV when the radio and the TV just stopped working. The radio was making a terrible noise and then the lights went off. It was so cold and we were stood there in the pitch black. I tried to feel my way to the window so I could open the blinds and curtains to let some street light in when

Anne screamed.

Anne: I shouted at Dai, "Don't move! It's in here with us."

Dai: That terrified me. It was like electricity in the hair. I could feel the hair on my arms and neck stand up, and even now thinking about it does the same. It was so bitterly cold. You could feel or sense this terrible presence when you just know. You just know there's something there with you.

Anne: The radio just blasted back on, just that clacking sound, and then the sound of a man, an animal, I couldn't tell, just making this deep moaning noise, like a hum, a deep hum, like when people are chanting.

Dai: The radio was really scaring me. I couldn't get to the window. Not that I was being held back, I just never seemed to be able to inch enough to it to let some light in. I shouted at Anne to turn that damn radio off and she said she was too frightened to move.

Anne: I shouted at Dai, "Open the window, open the door," but he said he couldn't. I think he was just as scared as I was. Then the lights came on and the TV and the radio came back on as if nothing had happened. Dai was stood by the bathroom door completely opposite from where the window was.

Dai: I have no idea how I ended up on the wrong side of the house. I felt like I had only taken a few steps towards the window. I was worried as when I was stood there in the dark I knew that huge figure was back, it was the same presence, the same feel to it.

Anne: Why it came in from the garden and through the house, I don't know. I'm not sure why it would be outside but I thought maybe it was showing us its power by walking through the house, affecting everything, showing itself, scaring us. It must have known we were not giving up the house, that we were getting someone in to get rid of it.

Dai: You knew it was in the house from there in. The presence was suffocating; you knew it was there watching you. The bathroom was freezing cold all the time and then the terrible smells would appear in pockets around the house, not like fart smells but something dead, something rotten.

Anne: It was the longest two days of my life waiting for Rose to come over. In my journal for 27th September 1990 I wrote:

I'm really struggling to cope, maybe I was wrong to try and fight this thing. Dai is down, he looks scared. We know it is back in the house. Dai said we should just go and wait until this woman comes to see us. I know we must be strong but I'm scared it is our fear that feeds it.

Today it is almost impossible to go into the bathroom. It is freezing and it smells like a dead animal in there. I am convinced this thing lives in there. I don't want to use the toilet or the shower.

Last night the storage room door opened and I could have sworn I could hear someone moving around downstairs. Dai is hardly sleeping as he said he can hear children downstairs singing. I have not heard that. Why do we see and hear different things?

2 more days and this will be over.

And then on the 30th September 1990, the day before Rose visited:

I asked Dai if we could stay in a hotel tonight. He is right. Last night while I was in the bathroom I saw in the mirror a reflection of a tall dark man figure with the head of an animal.

I think it was a dog's head. I can't take anymore. Nothing makes any sense anymore. I'm not clever enough to understand any of this, I never wanted this. I just want this gone. We are not bad people, we do not deserve this.

Dai told me to me to pack up and we are going to stay at a hotel. He is terrified. I am convinced we will die in this house if we stay here tonight.

Reading that back just takes my breath away. I did at that point think we were going to die. Overly dramatic? Yes, and people can laugh but nothing was making sense. I felt like we had been winning for a bit and now it was back stronger. I cannot tell you how or why I saw a figure with a dog's head; it might not have been a dog, but definitely an animal. Where was Dai? He was upstairs. He did ask if I wanted him to come down and wait while I was in there, but I foolishly said no. I thought if I ignored it and acted like nothing was happening then it would lose its power. It wasn't a man in a mask. From what I saw in the mirror it had a black body like a man, real black, and a head of an animal. I can't tell you much more than that.

Dai: When Anne told me we were going to a hotel, I was so relieved. I just wanted out. I would have slept in the car overnight rather than see what tricks the house had next for us. She told me about the dog-faced man and I couldn't say anything back. I didn't know what it was. Was it the Angry Man and the shadow dog as one or what? I'm not sure we are supposed to make sense of what it does. It's like a terrible dream that you have to live through, where nothing makes sense at all. I'm sure some shrinks could make some sense of it all; but until you live it, every day, in your face, then it's hard to just dismiss as something explainable.

Anne: We stayed at a hotel and we both felt relieved. For months I had felt drained, headaches, terrible stiffness in my neck, diarrhoea, my period out of sync, just generally out of sorts and Dai too was suffering from depression, migraines and had put on so much weight. I thought that this was it, the worst was behind us and after tomorrow it would be over. We didn't talk about the dog-headed man or the haunting or the dreams. We had dinner at the bar and a few drinks, and had some quiet time to ourselves that night.

Dai: The next day, I woke up and I felt so fresh like a huge weight was lifted off us. Before I was not one to believe in witchcraft and mediums, but I was open to anything plus just having someone in the house that could understand was a huge help. A problem shared is a problem halved.

Anne: Rose said she would meet us at five. We got there at four and we couldn't decide on whether we should just wait in the car or go in. I said let's go in. It was still light after all.

Dai: Looking back I would say most of the activity happened at night, there were the odd things in the day, but mainly at night.

Anne: Inside, the house always had this oppressive feel, like something bad had happened. You could just sense it. There was no smell on that day or anything when we went in, just that feeling. It was like when I was a young girl and I was late coming home from playing with my friends and I knew I would be in trouble with my mum. I would often have knots in my belly before entering the house.

Dai: Yeah, it was like: the house knew we were planning something.

Anne: Nothing downstairs was untoward other than the presence, until I noticed a spray of mould on the living room ceiling. I dashed upstairs expecting that maybe there was a leak coming from the ceiling and there was nothing. The bed was dry, carpet dry, windows closed. I didn't know at that time if this was something to do with the thing in the house or just damp. Rose would tell us what it was later and that was mind blowing.

Dai: The old woman, Rose, finally arrived around seven. I was worried that she would not turn up at all and dash our hopes of finishing this.

Anne: Rose was a lovely little old lady, and as soon as she came into the house, she stopped and said something terrible was here. She didn't ask any questions and immediately alluded to the mildew on the ceiling and said that this thing was hanging there like a spider. She told us what she could see was not anything like we could comprehend so she would describe it in a way that we could understand. She could see the entire room was a tangle of black vein-like roots growing and taking hold into our world. She said it was black, but it was actually even darker than what we could see in our world. It was a darkness that swallowed all the light. She said this was like nothing she had seen before, and turned to Dai and said she was *frightened*.

Dai: When she said she was frightened I just wanted to run out of the house. Apparently, she could see this other side where it lived and our house was like a nest for it and we were like flies in a web, and it would feed off our worry and fear and all the bad things we would think and do.

Anne: I asked her what could she do and she said the entity had used the negativity of dozens of people that had lived here before. She said one family, in particular, had done terrible things, those were the first, those were the ones that invited it in, and it drained them of the essence of what made them people. She explained it used them like puppets and they had never been allowed to pass on. They were still very much here, trapped inside its world. She said she could see glimpses of them contorted and rotten attached to huge black veins stemming from the thing on the ceiling. She said the children were almost unrecognizable. They were black twisted shapes, a blur of agony, and she almost made me sick when she said there was an older woman and the thing had many black tendrils inserted into her privates and she was vomiting or birthing little bits of blackness that would attach itself back to the main entity. It was growing.

Dai: A year before that I would laugh in her face, but at that time my hair was on end. It was like we had all taken a huge bag of drugs. I'm seeing our settee, our TV, and this old woman is seeing a world of blackened hell with old zombie women giving birth to little black blobs.

Anne: Rose told us that the entity would manifest into the shape of a tall shadow to interact physically in our world. It was hard to understand how, but it would put all its energy into that shape and that way it could move things in our world. It was a shadow of a man who had once lived there. He had been terrible and cruel, had hurt animals and children and was having an incestuous relationship with the old woman, his mother. The mother would make stew from animal corpses that the man would catch and kill. He was the one who opened the portal for this thing to come through. It was sickening and horrifying. Words cannot describe how disgusted I felt of that house. I wanted to burn it down.

Dai: Rose told Anne that she had been connecting with the man and had seen his world through his eyes. She had seen the house when the thing was first invading our world.

Anne: I had not told my friend about the dreams, and here was Rose telling me all about them. I didn't want to be connected to the Angry Man. It made me sick to think I had seen his mother have sex with him and Dai had seen a black shadow on me at the same time. How can this kind of thing even happen? Apparently, the Church had reached out to Rose before so they knew about it. They know there are things happening to people that shouldn't be happening. Do people in the government or scientists know about this? It makes me so angry to think how many people out there have suffered for so long and nothing is being done to stop it. I remember asking Rose what would happen if this thing was never stopped – what would happen – and she replied that it would spread and spread over decades into every room and then next door and then the street, and if there were people then it would feed on them. These things lurked all over the world waiting for people to break and leech from.

Dai: I asked her, "Would we end up like the family?" and she said they had died believing they could join it. It had tricked the man of the house and he was responsible for it all. When I investigated I did not find any evidence to suggest that a family of four were found dead at the house. Either it never happened or someone covered it up. I thought that maybe they were living there secretly and that is why no one knew of their deaths or what went on there. They must have had to venture outside at some point; someone must have known who they were. Four people dying at the same time in Haverfordwest in 1900 must have been noticed unless he killed them one at a time over a period. How could so many animals go missing without someone knocking on the door? I wish I had more answers.

Anne: I asked Rose, "What was it? Where had it come from?" And she said a place indescribable to us. It was not of spirit or our reality, something different and terrible. She felt that it was connected to a centre almost like it was part of something bigger again that was taking hold in little places all over the world. I didn't understand much. I'm not sure of a place outside our universe that not even God has control over.

Rose sat down and tears rolled down her face as she said what she was seeing was beyond Hell, and that she did not believe her methods could fight it off. The only thing she thought was to try and help the family cross and that way the thing would not be able to be energised and it would need new hosts or be forced to leave. She wasn't confident at all as the family was barely human; they were more of this thing than of people. They were the only way to stop this; they were the hosts that gave it energy. She looked at me; her eyes welled up and said she was sorry.

Dai: I asked her why she was sorry. It wasn't her fault and we would just move if this was real; and she said she was sorry because she could see skinny black tendrils attached to mine and Anne's heads like the rod on a bumper car. It was already taking a hold, it was draining us, making us ill, making us unhappy. She said it had taken hold of Anne; the worst and veiny black tendrils were already in her eyes and ears, spreading to her nose and mouth.

Anne: This sounds so stupid but I wanted to just hit her. Just hit this little old lady. I couldn't cope with this nonsense of who knows what from a place worse than Hell sucking the life from me with invisible tendrils stuck to my head. I just could not or would not accept it.

Dai: Anne got mad, the language she used, and the abuse she gave this old woman. I tried to calm her down. I told Rose to do whatever she must and she carried out some ritual. Anne sat on the settee, seething and swearing while I just imagined our living room all black and horrible, thinking, what the hell had happened to us? How did we get to this point? I did have doubts about Rose. I cannot prove or disprove what she claims to have seen and done as real. I knew the house was wrong and I was still hoping for a rational explanation, you know? Gas, drugs, military, something in the water, anything if it would just go away.

Anne: I can't remember much of what Rose did as I was so upset but she was burning different sticks and herbs, like Sunday dinner smell. She was making shapes on the floor with salt and using different candles and singing rhymes and songs, prayers I think. I just wanted to hurt her. I imagined ramming her head through the kitchen door. I think maybe the house was making me think like that. It was trying to stop her. I just can't understand how to describe this thing. It's not a ghost, it's not a demon. It's like a disease, an intelligent disease. Trying to understand it didn't make it any easier.

Dai: I thought of it like an alien virus, but then again, she said it was not from our universe. It was baffling. How can we describe something that we know nothing about?

Anne: I suddenly calmed down and started sobbing. Rose came from downstairs and she looked very ill and was dripping with sweat and said she had broken its bond in our world. She sat down as she said she thought she would faint. Dai ran and got her water and she told us that she could never do this again. That she thought it would kill her. It was more than she could handle again; but she looked at me and smiled and said I was free from it. I felt a surge of happiness go through my body. I believed her, I believed it had gone. We had our house back.

I hugged Rose and she said she had to do things that no one would do to remove it. She said there was a good power that invokes all that was light and positive in the world, but she said she had to use dark energy to fight this thing, a power she was ashamed of and something she would have to pay for later.

Dai: Did I think she had cleared our house. Hell knows? It was crazy. Little old ladies chucking salt around at something worse than evil and Anne wanting to chin an old woman while black webs were stuck to her head. I just went to Sir Thomas Picton School! I'm not a scientist or a professor. I just drive trucks for a living and fix cars now and again. I love football but barely understand the offside rule let alone all of this. I like a good pint and watching TV. I like a simple life. None of this made any sense.

Did I feel like anything had changed? Nothing, to be honest. Anne was smiling, she had colour in her cheeks. This little old lady was sweaty and smiling like she's done twelve rounds with Muhammad Ali, telling us she won and everything would be OK.

I wanted it to be over. I wanted to believe it was over. I needed Anne and me to have an ordinary life, no hauntings and newly discovered evils in our house. I just wanted us to be normal again. Pint and dinner on a Friday night, back to work, Anne and me happy. I would have done anything at that point to be happy again and for a time I was and then it came back and this time it went for me.

Congregation

Shall I, amidst a ghastly band, Dragged to the judgment-seat,
Far on the left with horror stand, my fearful doom to meet?
While they enjoy His heavenly love, Must I in torments dwell?
And howl (while they sing hymns above), and blow the flames of hell?

Charles Wesley's hymn *Terrible Thought! Shall I Alone* (1780)

I interviewed Dai and Anne over a two-year period, 46 interviews in total, and despite all the information they divulged, I regretted not being able to speak to Rose. Rose was a vital component to this case. Who was she and did she really have the gift of seeing other worlds layered over ours? I needed to know exactly what she saw.

I contacted every spiritualist church triangulated from Swansea to Cardigan to Pembroke, and no one could shed light on a lady called Rose who worked to expel unwanted presences from homes during this time. Had this woman worked hard to protect her identity or was she a fabrication created to add depth to Dai and Anne's paranormal testimonial?

I did not suspect the couple of acting deceitfully, but maybe they were embellishing their account as perhaps they thought it had little substance to this point. I personally found their account to be far more detailed and worrying than my own, and so much of what they disclosed connected to emotions I had believed I had overcome since my time at the house. There were things they spoke of that only someone who had experienced such an ordeal could speak of.

Finding more information on Rose was paramount, and in June 2017 I was contacted by a lady from Carmarthenshire who believed she knew who this enigmatic Rose was. I hastily travelled to meet my informant in person and she claimed that

Rose had existed but was not called Rose, which was her stage name so to speak. The lady had been prolific in the removal of such entities and had assisted the Church and the police on various matters.

Anonymity was cardinal to Rose as she was a staunch believer that gifts such as hers should not be used for profit and gain, and she held a very poor opinion of those that exploited their gifts or claimed to have powers when they did not. I, myself, had invited a so-called gifted person into the house during my experience who did nothing to help, and aggravated the activity. I approached this person for an interview for *A most haunted house* but they refused to answer any calls or comment on any questions. Sadly, there are those out there, damaging sorts, who exploit the very real needs of people looking for help and guidance on very challenging events in their lives.

Rose died in 1993 after a short but wrecking battle with cancer, and she had left her estate to the spiritual church she attended as she had little family left to bequeath her worldly possessions to. I was told she had a companion for her later years who was a dear friend that nursed her through ill health, who was elderly but still alive. I reached out to this lady requesting an audience so I could understand more of the work Rose conducted.

I met with Kathryn in Carmarthen town centre and was delighted to meet a spritely lady in her early 80s. She was tireless and energetic, enthusiastic to discuss Rose. They had met at the spiritual church in the late 60s and had become very close friends. Kathryn described their relationship as more family than mere friends. Kathryn, obviously younger than Rose, felt a maternal bond had been forged, a bond she thought lost after the death of her own mother to suicide.

Rose had been prevalent in many haunting, demonic and criminal cases since the 1950s. Rose had participated in so many cases that a huge volume on her life alone would still not be an adequate recording of the life she led. It was a remarkable existence. She had shunned fame and fortune and lived a very puritan life, a life rewarded for the help for others. Rose was indeed exceptionally gifted to the degree that she was a trusted authority to both the legal and Christian establishments.

I asked Kathryn if she could recall the incident in Haverfordwest in the autumn of 1990. Kathryn's sparkling eyes dulled as she explained that was Rose's final assignment before she retired and fell into ill health. Kathryn said that Rose was never the same again and had believed she had lost her power, her gift, as result of her visit to the house. Whatever had happened that day, Rose had manifested all her capabilities into dispersing the presence that lived there.

I was desperate to gain a better understanding of what the presence was. Based on Dai and Anne's testimonial it had absorbed and contorted monstrously the family from a century previous, but what effect would it have short term on the likes of Dai, Anne and myself? I had been a victim of depression, dependency and tried to take my own life. Did I and others that had resided there still have a link, a connection to the darkness at the house? Would we be able to simply move on and enjoy life? What fate awaited us after our final life force flickered off and we departed the material world? Were we damned also?

Kathryn had said that Rose had broken down after the investigation at Haverfordwest and rarely conversed on the happening. What Kathryn could recall was a conversation she had before Rose died. Rose confessed to having done something terrible to release the hold on the house and that her spirit would find no peace after death. Kathryn has no clue to what incantation or ritual Rose had performed. Had she called on power from an ancient and more terrible world to combat this new threat? Rose was frightened; she did not want to die as she believed that not a Heaven nor a Hell waited for her but the darkness. She would find no peace after death, only suffering.

Hell, as we imagined it, Kathryn explained to me, was not fire and brimstone but a place of sadness, solitude and anguish. Hell is a feeling, a feeling that you will never be able to escape from; a cold and lonely place for those that found no joy in life, trapped in the shadows of life. However, what Rose was fearful of was real ceaseless suffering; physical, emotional and mental torture that her contact with this indescribable entity ensured. Seconds would feel like lifetimes and every contact with the darkness would be an eternal damnation, a rotting of the soul. Every pain, every anguish, every suffering imaginable amplified a billion-fold with no hope of escape. She had poked it, provoked it and now she would suffer.

There was nothing to compare to it. It had no name, no language, no face, no true form and we could never understand its origin. These are concepts that would snap our minds. This was beyond Heaven and Hell. This was beyond good and evil, God and Satan. Kathryn enlightened me that these deities were specks of sand on a beach compared to the power of the darkness that resides in the shadow, waiting in the blackness, waiting to take a foothold in our lives. God did not create it, God had no domain over it and the Devil feared it.

This is a very challenging concept on many levels. We would have to believe that there is a God, the creator and ruler of the universe and source of all moral authority – the Supreme Being who created everything we know – but did not create this dark existence. Therefore, does a source more powerful than God exist, and if so how did it come into being? However, if you do not believe God exists and did not create the universe then where has this entity emerged from? Is it an alien species or a dimensional presence, or is it from an unfathomable place not yet discovered by mankind, a place different to our own universe? Are we contemplating parallel universes, other dimensions, or a theory yet undiscovered? How are we supposed to classify what we can't comprehend?

Kathryn and I visited Rose's grave and stood there looking

at a physical testament to her life. A forgotten soldier, who had braved battles with the unknown, with ghosts and demons and of all the things that haunt this world. She had found peace for many, eased crossings into the light and had perhaps sacrificed her own peace to battle something she was not equipped to defeat.

Staring at the headstone made me fearful of my own mortality.. I had no children to nurture and love, to continue my legacy, and I felt the sands of times slipping away from my time on Earth. I had wasted so much time entrenched in misery. I started to contemplate my morbid pursuits of the paranormal. Maybe I needed to reconsider ideas of dark entities from a place we cannot see or understand, and think about starting a family and hang up my investigator's hat. Who was I to try and figure this all out? How arrogant was I to address such gigantic concepts as the origins of this entity, its purpose and its command over us? Who was I to question the fabric of the universe, the validity of a creationist God and the prospect of life after death?

I am just a man, raised on the Merlin's Bridge Council Estate, self-educated and afflicted with dyslexia, trying to piece together an unsolvable puzzle that no self-respecting scientist would give a moment's thought to. What if I could prove all of this, who would accept it? I felt that maybe myself, Dai, Anne and the others had luckily escaped its grasp, and now it was time to put the experience behind us and just live a happy life till we take that final breath, the sweetest breath of all.

I stared down, a sadness welling inside, at her final resting place. I had many questions that would go unanswered but a seed was planted in my mind, a seed that told me to step away and leave it be, finish the project and move on and never let thoughts of that damned house consume me again. The theories of a long-departed lady could not diminish the lust for life I had been granted after my time in the house. It was over for me. The house regardless of what happening there was just a house. I didn't have to return there. I was not a slave to its command and as I thought this Kathryn said solemnly:

> *Rose did not banish that thing, you know. She never defeated it, she confessed before she died. It chewed on her soul. It showed her something terrible. There is no way anything can defeat it. She just stopped it growing for a bit. That was all.*

Anne: I definitely felt the house was better after Rose's visit. The air, the mood – it all changed. I was worried of course that it could come back, but it seemed fresher somehow. I believed at that time that Rose had defeated it; you see exorcists and mediums in films and TV cleanse a property, and that's what I thought she did. Even my thoughts were calmer and happier. I didn't want to think what it was or where it had come from. I just wanted it gone and gone for good.

Dai: We couldn't see what Rose could see, the other world. I'm not even sure what she did to get rid of it. Was it a performance or did she believe she could remove ghosts and demons or whatever we had? We don't even have a name for it. Where do you start? The darkness, the blackness, the thing? The house did seem different after her visit, I can't deny that at all, and for a while things were good.

Anne: After a quiet night, we went to the pub the next evening and talked about what had happened and what we should do next. Dai suggested we should just sell up and move on, but I convinced him the house was OK now and Rose had fixed it all. I felt better. I slept the best I had in ages. Everything was better. Dai was just a little defensive. Who could blame him?

Dai: I said if anything, and I mean anything, happened over the next week, month even, then we would be gone, no talking, no quarrelling. We would pack up and leave and look to sell. I couldn't handle all that again. It might have been something paranormal or it might have been something rational. Either way, it's not good to be living like that, stressed, frightened and depressed. I had never been like that before, and until your book, we didn't know of anyone either.

Anne: Dai was signed off to go back to work early with light duties in October 1990 and that helped him and us so much. It did him the world of good to get out of the house, see his friends, and start earning money again. I worked the pub and picked up more hours as Christmas was coming up and the house was quiet. The house was just a house again. One thing I never brought up earlier was how quickly food turned and went off in the house before Rose's visit. Flowers would die and fruit would rot. I'm not sure if that was anything to do with the house at all but after Rose, the food never spoiled, well for a few months at least.

Dai: It was great to be back in work. The lads joked at how fat I was, calling me Fatty Bum Bum and Jabba the Hutt and I didn't mind. You develop very thick skin after the year we had and I was just glad to be around people, to be useful, to laugh and joke again. It was a great tonic to take my mind off everything. It had been a traumatising time.

Anne: Christmas came and I did think back to the year before. That was when the activity started to build up so I did have little concerns, but for two months nothing happened, nothing at all.

Dai: Months passed and nothing happened. One thing happened Christmas Eve, but it wasn't physical, it wasn't something in the house as such. It was a dream I had that worried me. We continued our tradition of a Christmas Eve in the pub and we had a few pints. Anne and I decided we would not talk about what had happened again. Sounds daft but we didn't want to tempt fate as if talking about it would bring it back. The house had been great for months and life was good again. Anne and I had a better relationship, if anything. We had been through so much, nearly broke up and gone through Hell and come out the other side stronger.

There was no need to sleep with the lights on or have tape recorders recording on the landing; it was all in the past, unforgettable yeah, but in the past. I had drunk a few pints and got into bed and dropped off as soon as I got into bed. The last thing I remember was laughing at Anne, only in her underwear, as she tried to take off my boots for me and she was falling over trying to do it, giggling and telling me to shush.

I had a terrible dream. In my dream, I woke up and I was awake in bed just staring at the ceiling. I could just make it out in the gloom with the street light coming in from behind the blinds and curtain. I don't know why I was staring at the ceiling. I was worried that there was something there. In my head, I said, *"Who's there? What do you want?"*

There seemed to be a hatch, maybe an attic door, which is not there or was not there when we lived there. I'm staring at this black hole in the ceiling when I sensed something moving up there.

I said again, *"Who's there? What do you want?"*

I watched a pair of dark hands stretch down, big long hands, attached to skinny arms. I remember being so scared; scared these hands would grab me or strangle me. The arms stretched and stretched, incredibly long, impossibly long till they were inches from my face. I tried to push my head deeper into my pillow. I was too frightened to get out of bed. I couldn't scream, I couldn't will myself to just run. The fingers touched my face, they were cold and clammy and they smelt of rotten meat. The fingers were feeling my face. I shut my eyes and my mouth tight as they tried to pry them open. I thought they would gouge out my eyes or stretch down my throat. In my head, I was screaming for it to stop. I was begging. I was threatening to kill it. I was crying for my mother. I felt those cold stinking fingers feel into my nose and push inside. They stretched and stretched deeper up my nose and the pain was awful. I thought they would push into my brain and kill me.

Anne: Dai woke me up. He was screaming, flat on his back screaming. I turned on the light and he was just staring at the ceiling screaming. I was terrified. I shook him and he stopped and stared at me.

Dai: Anne was terrified, just staring at me, and the first thing she asked was, "Has it come back?" I remember asking her if I was awake and she said I was and asked again. I lied to her; I told her I had a nightmare about crashing my lorry. She looked so relieved. Why did I lie? Because that night I had no idea if it was the house or just a bad dream. It was terrifying and it felt so real. I thought I had felt the pain but it didn't fit the activity that had happened over the year. I hoped, I prayed it was just a dream but as you'll find out it wasn't. It was back.

Anne: Dai said it was just a nightmare and not to do with the house. I didn't want it back. It was Christmas and life was very good, best it had been in years.

Dai: A few days later, it was before New Year, we had come back from a family get-together and there was a film I wanted to watch on TV. I used to love to get the *Radio Times* and circle the films I wanted to watch over Christmas; maybe tape a few to keep. Anne was on the phone and I nipped in for a quick shower.

I was in the shower, and as I got to leave and open the door through the mist and the water I saw someone in the bathroom just staring at me. I thought it was Anne, but it was shorter and in a brown dress. I opened the door, and in the time I did this the figure was gone.

I grabbed a towel and went into the living room and Anne was lying on the settee, still on the phone. She looked at me and she stopped smiling.

Anne: I remember clearly that night Dai had come out of the bathroom like he had seen something. I got goosebumps and I felt a twisting in my stomach. He lied, of course, he lied to protect me and he said he thought he heard someone knocking on the door.

Dai: I didn't want it to be back. I hoped that it was just some flashback. You hear of people who have been in stressful conditions, in accidents, and they still see things and feel things. I was still hoping it was just that.

Anne: I asked him if that was the case and he said, yeah. He was shaking but he said it was because he was wet and cold and he went upstairs and dried himself. I knew deep down it was back, but I hoped that was it, just a quick reminder it had been there and then we would never see it again.

Dai: Things were quiet for a bit, again, as it would and late January I was in the kitchen making a cuppa when the radio turned itself on. There was a lot of static and then a high-pitched noise. I thought to myself, here we go, it's happening again. Anne was working and I thought if it's back we need to go. I was feeling frightened and depressed again. I thought, what if we can't escape this? What if it follows us wherever we go? I started to not feel myself and I thought mad things, terrible things that make me so ashamed. I thought maybe Anne and I would have to commit suicide to escape it. How mad? Where does that come from?

Anne: Dai sheepishly told me the radio was on the blink again and I said I would take it back, and he said he didn't think Alabaster's could help. I was very angry with him. I blamed him if it was back. I wrongly thought that his weakness, his dwelling on the thing had brought it back. I slapped him so hard. He took it, he didn't fight back, he didn't say a word. He just headed up to bed and I shouted after him that he was wrong. It was all in his head, and the way it was going it was going to come back and it would be all his fault.

Dai: She blamed me. She said if it came back it was all my fault so I better buck up and get positive. She said positive thoughts were our best weapon. What a load of nonsense. I went to bed and thought about going downstairs and just throwing her out. I was so angry I thought about punching her. Looking back, it was starting to take hold over us again. I had thoughts of suicide, violence and anger.

Anne: The next day we had a huge argument. I told him that it was probably him that made it all happen. He had probably drugged me, made me think I had gone mad and now he was trying it again.

Dai: Anne blamed me and I said some awful things. I told her what a cow she was and I wish I had been having an affair last year so at least I wouldn't have to put up with her nonsense anymore. I was so angry. My mood affected work. I was rude and unpleasant to my friends.

I convinced myself then that Anne was seeing someone at her work, maybe one of the patrons, so I started following her to work, spying on her. I thought all the time of her sleeping with someone else and it tore me up. When she blamed me I started to think, no, she was behind it all, the house. Maybe she had switched up my medication, put something in my food. What an awful time. I cringe thinking about it now.

Anne: We were on the brink of breaking. We were very hateful of each other. Nothing happened in the house for a while. I think the house was using us; we were the ones acting crazy and awful. It was like it had a hold of us.

The night before our last ever night, Valentine's 1991 of all days, was the night. That was the turning point. I had been finding it hard to sleep and I had something niggling in mind for a few weeks but things were so bad between Dai and I that we barely spoke. We didn't exchange cards or anything. We barely spoke. We shared the same bed but not in an intimate way. To be honest, I think we shared the bed because we feared the house. I wanted to talk to him but he had shut me out. I finally fell asleep, and in my dream, I had returned to the house as it was back in the past.

I was stood in the bedroom. I didn't feel paralysed like before. I felt like I was in control. It was how it had been the day the old woman crawled on top of me. There was no carpet, wooden floorboards and it was cold in there. I looked out of the window but it was too dirty, too blurry to see out, but what I could make out was not the road and cars I was used to, but a smaller track, a smaller-looking road.

I felt myself moving towards the door. I opened it and stood on the landing. There was no light, just the light from behind me. I could hear muffled voices behind the storage room door and I opened it up. It was dark in there but I could make out two little children sat in there. There was a boy and a girl, the boy was maybe nine or ten, the girl a bit younger. Both were dirty and unkempt and both had a dirty cloth, like a blindfold, over their eyes. I wanted to reach out to them, to undo their blindfolds but I couldn't will myself to do it.

The little girl lifted her head towards me and said, *"She's back, don't move, Kenneth, she's back."* He whimpered and hid his head into her shoulder and said, *"Make her go away, please make her go away."*

I found myself moving away from them and down the stairs into what was our dining room, but in the dream, it was a room with dark furniture, a big dresser and a big cabinet and lots of boxes. It looked like a room that was being used for storage or needed to be unpacked. The kitchen door was open and I headed in. It was bigger than it was now, twice as wide with a door to the right. On an old stove was a steaming big metal pan. I felt the need to look at it. I peered over it and inside boiling away was what I could only describe as a skinned cat. The smell was sickening. I wanted to wake up. I wanted to scream. I didn't want to be here. I wanted to run away.

I turned and headed to where our living room is now. I thought if only I could make it on to the street. Maybe I could find help. I opened the door and the living room was smoky. The window had been boarded up and there were streaks of light coming through the gaps. There was a big fire burning and sat on a table chair was a big man, broad shouldered, dark hair, dark beard, and his legs long and spread, and between his legs, kneeling, facing him was the old woman in brown. She was making this awful slurping sound. I don't think I should describe what she was doing to him but it was disgusting. I knew this was the cruel man and this was his sick mother, and what they were doing was wrong. How sick were these people? What had they done to the children? Why were they cooking cats?

She stopped and she turned and looked straight at me. She opened her mouth, her teeth black as she hissed at me, *"Your baby will make for a lovely broth."*

I woke up and I didn't scream, I didn't panic. I was very calm. It was back and it was going to be worse because it wasn't just Dai and me now. There were three of us to think of. I was pregnant.

Dai: Anne didn't tell me about the dream until the day after our final night. I had dreamt of the arms grabbing for me but I guess I was blessed to only dream that. I'm not sure if what Anne saw in her dreams were real clues to work on but I never found any information on them and could not find a Kenneth that died around that time. 15th February 1991 was the final night we lived in that house.

Anne had been very quiet all day. My angry thoughts of affairs and hatred had been replaced with sadness and self-loathing. I hated myself. I just wanted to drink myself to death if I'm honest. Whereas before I had fight and energy to leave the house, sell it, burn it down, whatever it took to be free of it, at that time I just wanted to curl up and die. I wanted Anne to find me dead and feel awful for how she had treated me. I wanted her to have that guilt on her for the rest of her life.

I blamed her more than the house. I started to forget what the house had done and just put all the blame on her. I couldn't snap out of it. I was even writing suicide notes in my head. I felt I would teach her. Stupid, right?

The final ever night I was in bed, Anne had gone to sleep. We had not said a word to each other all day. She had gone to work. I had phoned in sick. I was lying there thinking of dying and how everyone would miss me. How they wished they had been better to me, appreciated me, all this daft shit, when I got up as I needed a pee.

I got up and didn't even think about being scared of the house. I just headed off in the dark, and when I got to the landing I could hear this strange noise. It reminded me of cows breathing, like heavy phuff, phuff noises coming from downstairs.

Why I headed down I cannot say but I slowly went down the stairs and I just kept imagining something grabbing my leg. I got to the bottom and peered into the living room and there in the centre of the room, illuminated by the light coming in through the window, were these shapes, black solid shapes. They were making this phuff noise in unison. It was a strange heavy breathing noise like when people hyperventilate.

These shapes were congregated around one large figure, a figure I had seen before. I get goosebumps and a dread in my stomach thinking of it now. It was freezing downstairs and I was just stood there in my pants and T-shirt, frozen, unable to move, watching this horrible sight.

The tall figure was stood there with a smaller figure, around five feet and again two smaller figures; they were shadows no bigger than a child and darker than the darkness of the room. The breathing noises they made were making my blood turn to ice. Even now I can hear it in my head as if I am still there.

I'm not sure how long I watched this. I wasn't dreaming before you ask. This was real. As real as seeing you in front of me. The more I listened to the breathing the more I wanted to join the congregation, the more I wanted to give in and let myself go. I think I was ready to do that and am not sure what would have happened if I had, but I kept thinking of Anne. How we were when we first met, our first kiss, our first night together, how much I love her.

I quickly reached and turned on the light and ran upstairs. I was so noisy that I'm not sure when the breathing noises stopped. I woke Anne up. I was shouting for her to get up.

Anne: He ran into the room, shouting, but not at me in an angry way but in a way to wake me up. He was wild eyed and said over and over that he loved me. He was sorry. I couldn't get him to calm down and then he looked me in the eyes and said, "We have to go now," and that's when I told him I was pregnant.

Dai: When she told me that then it was clear – we had to go now. No more trying to fight it or live with it. No more trying to figure out what it was. We just had to go.

Anne: And we left in the middle of the night. We grabbed a few clothes and we sped off from the house and drove for miles. As I left the house, seeing all our stuff there, running in the middle of the night I felt a calm. But as I left, I could see from the corner of my eye a black blur just unfold from the kitchen ceiling and drop to the floor. I closed the door and we left.

Dai told me over and over how much he loved me, how sorry he was and was so happy we would have a baby together. I don't know how much he told me he would be the best dad ever, and he has been. I started laughing and crying as I was so happy we were together. This weight lifted off us. The badness just melted. We had freed ourselves.

Dai: It gets me now. How close we were to losing each other. I love her so much, I'm proud of that. I love her and we made a beautiful family. We had a healthy baby girl. I am the proudest dad you can imagine. People talk about soulmates and Anne is mine. What happened there brought us closer together, made us stronger, and made us appreciate each other and life again. I'm so sad what happened to you, Gavin, when you lived there. I wish you could have had the happy ending we did.

Anne: What did we do? We stayed at my mum's for a bit, and oddly enough a flat above work came up for rent. Small little place but we moved in there. It was tight money-wise, but we put the house on the market and eventually sold it.

Dai: Did we tell the people that moved there about what had happened? No, not directly. Does that make us bad people? Not at all as we did do something, well Anne did.

Anne: I wrote an anonymous letter and put it through the door months later. The letter said that we used to live in the house decades before, you know, put them off the scent and that we thought some bad things lived in the house. I said if things got bad to just go, but hoped it was a happy house for them. Can you imagine waking up to that letter?

I walked past the house often before we moved south of the county. They did a lot of work to the house but every year or so it would be back up for sale. I think it's empty now. I hope so. How many people have gone through that? How many people hearing this are realising that was the house they lived in?

Reflection

Many have puzzled themselves about the origin of evil. I am content to observe that there is evil, and that there is a way to escape from it, and with this, I begin and end.
John Newton

The interviewing process had taken two years to complete, and finally, the testament was concluded. Dai and Anne had felt the cathartic release that I had experienced for unburdening myself from the grasp of secrecy. It was an emotional period where two ordinary people relived a terribly confusing and horrific time with more questions veiled behind the answers in an unsolvable puzzle.

I grew to admire and appreciate this Pembrokeshire couple's strength. How not only had they survived but thrived, forging a loving life of family and happiness. Where I had been alone to decipher my experiences, tangled in the shadowy clutches of the house, they had each other. Two people sharing a common trauma, both able to share in the inexplicable experience, both working together to overcome the derangement of such an awful period of their lives.

It was comforting to me to share notes and ideas with them on what had happened. Neither Dai nor I had come any closer to discovering more about the previous occupants of the house. Had such a morally-corrupted family lived in that house at the turn of the twentieth century? No evidence of such people had been uncovered at this time, but the digging will continue.

Dai and Anne were satisfied with the telling of their part in the history of that infamous abode, and were content to leave behind an experience that no one, confidently, can explain. We had agreed upon completion of the account and before publishing that we have one final interview; a final opportunity to reflect on their time at the house in Haverfordwest and an occasion for final questions.

GL: Now that the interview is over after two very arduous years of questioning, and having to relive your experience, how do you feel about the prospect of the world hearing your testimonial?

Anne: I know some people will be worried by it and some will call us liars, but we know what happened to us and for them to think we are liars then I take that as a blessing that nothing bad like this has happened to them.

Dai: It's been a hard two years, to be honest. You really pushed us to relive it and bring us back to the house which I guess is your job and you are very good at it, but it's been hard so I'm relieved. I'm glad we did it. It felt for a time that we were back and a lot of bad memories came back. It is crazy how much is vividly stored in our brains. Some nights I would go to bed and feel like we were still back in the house.

GL: What would you say, Dai, to people that think this is made-up?

Dai: I'd say well, good for you, you obviously know everything there is to know about everything. In ten, maybe twenty years' time when the human race discovers something new or something different from how we thought, then I will remind them again, you obviously know everything there is to know about everything, even before it changes.

GL: Did you have any strange dreams, visions or happenings while discussing the house for this testimony?

Anne: I had a few dreams but nothing near as vivid as back in the house.

GL: What kind of dreams?

Anne: Just anxiety dreams that I was back in the house. One was awful where I felt I was locked in the house and it was dark and I couldn't get out.

Dai: Same for me. Just dreams I was in the house in the dark and something was there, but then you wake up and you realise you are back in your home and it's a happy and safe place.

GL: I know that you, Dai, had the dream with those long arms, but Anne seemed to have more of a connection to the house through her dreams. Her dreams were more intense and prolific. Why do you think this was the case?

Anne: In later years I have learnt that I am more spiritually attuned, not gifted as some are, but I do feel positive and healing energy so I think maybe I had tapped into that back then without realising it. Maybe I was more vulnerable; maybe it just found me easier to connect to.

Dai: I think I was trying to block so much of it out, looking for rational explanations, and of course I was on medication and drinking so for a time I slept like a log. That dream with the arms was enough. When we were talking about it, I could still feel those fingers on my face. It had the feel of wet mushrooms, horrible.

GL: Has anything happened over the last 25 years in this house which has made you think it's followed you here?

Dai: Nothing at all, it's such a different place. When the sun is shining and the estuary is blue and calm and even the lights of the refinery are beautiful in its own way, there is just a sense of peace here.

Anne: We raised two children here and it's been such a happy place. A million miles apart, if that house was Hell then this house is Heaven. We have had a lot of happy times and not only the kids but grandkids too.

GL: You described this house as Heaven and the other place as Hell. Is that what you think it was? A place of evil? Was it a demonic being that tormented you?

Anne: Rose had said it was beyond Hell, a place that we have not discovered yet. It boggles my mind to this day. On TV they discover new planets and things in the universe, and I think is it something to do with all that. Rose could see a world different from ours that was evil and destroying, but I always imagined Hell as fire and the Devil; but the house was a black like a disease. She said it was something we can't even imagine.

Dai: I did some reading into it and there are places so far in the universe that even we can't see it and we don't know what's there. Also I tried to follow multiverse theories and parallel dimensions and I can't fully understand it. It's beyond my comprehension. I just drive lorries.

Anne: I think it was Hell though. Maybe that is Hell. Maybe Rose was just seeing a new version of Hell. I don't know.

GL: How do you feel that Rose, I don't want to say lied, but embellished her capacity to rid you of this thing in the house?

Dai: Whatever she did in all fairness did stop it for months, a good two months. I don't know what she did. She frightened us and I don't know if she had powers or not, you know gifts? That was a mad night. I thought Anne was going to hit her. She wasn't acting when she said she was scared. It wasn't nice seeing an old lady in your house telling you it's the worst house she has ever seen.

Anne: I'm not upset with Rose as I felt she did help and she tried her best. It was not as if we could get the police involved and she was the best option we had. I was told even the Church used her.

GL: Rose was said to have assisted the Church with cases similar to yours. Do you think that people higher up know about this kind of phenomena, and if so why aren't they supporting and helping people like you?

Dai: The Catholic Church has exorcists and so much in the Bible is supernatural if you think about it. They know the truth but they can't admit to it, as people would panic. The police use psychics and dowsers to solve crimes. They know but they can't admit it as it shows we aren't in control of the world.

Anne: So many people have had experiences of the paranormal and Dai is right. The Bible is full of paranormal things and strange events and no one bats an eyelid; but if you say you have ghosts then you are mad. Royalty, famous people, professional people have all said they have seen ghosts or had strange encounters, so why would they make it up? I think sceptics have been brainwashed not to believe or be frightened of what really might be out there.

GL: So, do you believe an entity, force, darkness, whatever we choose to label it, has the power to affect us emotionally, make us feel and do terrible things?

Anne: Definitely, one hundred per cent. I know we can suffer from depression and stress, but this was something different. I had such awful thoughts. I was convinced Dai was having an affair. I pushed my mum away. I nearly lost my job. I was an awful person and I've never been like that before or after. I've had down bouts, of course, but not like that.

I'm not trying to make excuses for people as there are really bad people out there; but what if some of the bad things in life like depression, suicide, violence, abuse, sexual perverts, an addiction even murder is caused by one of those things. I changed living with it, so did Dai, so did you, so did your girlfriend. It does affect people.

Dai: I nearly lost my mind. I wanted to hit Anne at one stage. I too thought she was having an affair. I was depressed, miserable, overweight and by the end suicidal. I would never hit anyone. I'm not prone to depression and thoughts of suicide. If you think rationally then I was on pain medication, drinking and sleep patterns all over the place so that could be to blame; but by the end, I was a madman and as soon as we left I felt better. Not over a few weeks but immediately.

GL: I have to ask this and it may be a little upsetting but it will be a question that people will want answered. You conceived your daughter in the house during a time where it may be possible that something otherworldly was cohabiting with you. Did you ever worry that she might have been different, affected somehow?

Anne: I did on that last night there. I had visions of a demon baby or the stress of it all resulting in a miscarriage or stillbirth, just something terrible. But once we left the house I knew we were alright.

Dai: No, but there was no way you could raise a baby in that house. Who knows what would have happened to it. Our daughter is beautiful, wonderful, bright, fun-loving and now a new mum herself and nothing has ever made me think there was something wrong with her.

GL: How much do your children know of this?

Anne: They know we lived in a haunted house in Haverfordwest. We never went into details. Now they keep asking why a writer keeps coming to the house. We have told them more about it but not all of it.

Dai: They will certainly know when the book comes out but we will talk to them first about it. It's part of our life before they were born and nothing for them to worry about. They might think we are mad but I think they already think that.

GL: If you had to give the thing at the house a name what would you call it?

Anne: I called it the darkness, but the thing is the most common.

Dai: I always associated it with the tall shadow that you called the Angry Man, so I called it the shadow thing the most, darkness, shadows or the presence.

GL: I have felt incredibly guilty over the last decade for not warning people in the house of what lurks there. I, like you, wrote a letter to the occupants that lived there once. Do you think we have a responsibility to warn people of what resides there?

Dai: I think about this a lot. Anne wrote a letter and so did you plus you wrote a book on it and I guess if anyone lives there and is experiencing it then, surely, they would have looked online and read *A most haunted house* or the articles on your website. In my day, there was no Internet and I had no one to talk to about it other than Anne. You left, we left. So if it gets that bad then I'm sure they will leave.

Anne: I wrote a letter and I have been tempted to knock on the door and talk to whoever lives there. It looks empty now. Didn't you say that over seven people lived there from 1991 to 2003 and at least twelve more people since? I agree with Dai that if something bad is happening there then they will find the book. I heard about the book in work and contacted you. It's probably the most read-about paranormal book about Pembrokeshire ever written.

GL: Would you destroy, demolish the house if you could?

Dai: In a heartbeat. I'd burn it down. Grind the remains into dust and drop them into the middle of the sea.

Anne: No. How do you know if you demolish the house that it won't just move to another house, or get into the atmosphere and be worse? The house is empty; leave it that way. No people to feed off.

GL: Do you believe the family seen in dreams, the ones Rose spoke about, are real people?

Anne: I can't tell you why and I can't prove it, but I believe that family existed and lived in that house. My dreams were so vivid, so real, and unless you have experienced it then it is hard to explain. The dream and what Rose said along with what we saw and felt convinced me they were real.

Dai: I think if all of this is real, to which it's not gas or drugs or something in the water or the air there, then they are real. I can't find any evidence mind you to say they are real, but I'm sure what I saw that last night was the four of them doing that weird breathing stuff in the living room. They were terrifying in death and who knows what they got up to in life. Incest, animal cruelty, child abuse and who knows what else, satanic rituals? We are not like that. We have raised a good family. We love our children and our pets. We could not make all that up. Anne couldn't invent such awful things as that.

Anne: I think regardless of what we think caused it, whether it was this terrible undiscovered place or Hell, I genuinely think that family haunted that house. Maybe they did invite something in, opened a portal, but I think they were terrible people, to begin with, and they are the key to all of this.

GL: Dai, despite everything you witnessed, everything you saw and felt, everything that Anne endured, you still deep down believe there is a rational explanation to all of this?

Dai: You have to, don't you? It's not right to believe in all these things. I know what we saw and felt and it was terrifying but I still hold on to what if we were poisoned or drugged? What if there was something in the water or the air? Maybe someone spiked the water, I don't know. I often think about gas seeping in from under the house. There are old mines down in Hook and Llangwym that sometimes cave in under houses and gardens, and what if there was one under that house seeping out a gas or chemical? I even thought a lot about the military. You said in *A most haunted house* that they had been testing out a new communications device that was an old Cold War weapon used to demoralise troops. What if they had been testing this years before they said they were?

Anne: I think that would be too coincidental to make everything rational and not just us but you too, Gavin. How many people have suffered at that house? Maybe Dai is right. In my gut, though, my intuition tells me that something very wrong was attached, was living in that house and it affected us. We felt it, you and your ex-girlfriend felt it and so did Rose. It's too many coincidences for it to be something explainable.

GL: I have done much study into psychological conditions that could be responsible for it that may back Dai's theory, such as Toxic Mould Syndrome [*See possible explanations and causes at the end of this book.*], which has been given much merit as a possible cause of paranormal phenomena. How do you feel about that?

Dai: I read your article on it and it could very well be behind it.

Anne: Rose was in the house a few seconds before she started seeing what she did. If it was a mould then how come your experience was different to ours, how come it would go quiet for months at a time? I don't think it was. I truly believe that something paranormal is happening at that house.

GL: You said you had evidence, pictures of a face in the headboard, Polaroids of the house from that time and recordings of noises on the landing. People may find it very convenient that they were lost. What are your thoughts on that?

Anne: We moved so quick, all of it was in a shoebox and I swore they were packed, but to be honest once we settled down again I really didn't want to listen to or see all that again. If we still had it then we would have given it to someone like you to study.

Dai: Even if we had the box the people could still say we faked it all or give rational explanations. I have no idea how that box went missing. We rushed out of there and it must have been left behind or lost. Someone somewhere had seen that box and must have thought, "What are all these strange pictures and tapes?" If anyone has them, contact Gavin and I will pay a reward for them.

GL: What would you say you have taken from this experience? How has it affected your life?

Anne: I'm happy we escaped. I'm happy we told you. I'm happy we have had the life we have had. It was a terrible time and at times I thought we would lose each other, even die. We came through and it didn't beat us. We are stronger and happier than we have ever been. I'm not religious at all, but I'm more spiritual. I joined a spiritual church and I feel more connected to the good things in life, nature, people, my feelings. I feel joy in so much. I feel appreciation and I feel that there are positive forces out there that do protect us. In the strangest way possible it was the best thing that ever happened to us.

Dai: I am so grateful for what we have. We are blessed with a beautiful family, friends, life and each other. There was a time when I thought we would lose it all.

GL: I would very like to buy the house. Would you ever step inside the house again?

Dai: No, never. Knock it down as I said.

Anne: I couldn't, not again. It almost broke us. I think it would have ended up very tragic if we had. Dai would have done himself in and who knows what would have happened to me. Can you imagine trying to raise a baby in that house? The old woman threatened to eat the baby! It's over now. Telling you, knowing people will read this, means it's over.

GL: Before we conclude our final interview, I have one thing I would like you to listen to. [*I play them* Go Get the Ax.]

Dai: That's a bit of a shock, everything rushed back to me. I never thought I would hear that again. What an awful time of our life.

Anne: Can you turn it off, please? I don't want to hear that in this house ever.

GL: Imagine, if you will, someone is reading this and they realise it's the house they are living in and realise it's happening to them. What message do you have for them?

Dai: Get out, leave now, grab your stuff and never go back. Don't take any chances. Don't wait for it to get better. No one can help you. Just go.

Anne: Get out, get out, get out, and get out now!

Interview 46 concluded 19th May 2017.

Coupling

> *You gain strength, courage, and confidence by every experience in which you really stop to look fear in the face. You are able to say to yourself, "I lived through this horror. I can take the next thing that comes along."*
> Eleanor Roosevelt

It was a bittersweet farewell to two people who had become more than subjects of a book. They had accepted me as a friend over the years I had conducted the interviews. I had sat and enjoyed dinner with their family and felt part of something very special. They were people who understood what I had dealt with alone for a decade. However, with the interview over I could commit the transcript to book form and no longer have to dread any new revelations of their time there at least for a while.

They had been generous with their time and asked for nothing in return but to have an open mind listen to and record their account. Dai and Anne would get back to their lives, to their family, while I sat alone with piles of notes and recordings trying to make sense of not only their experience but mine also.

Whereas you may be relieved to know their experience from 1989 to 1991 had ended, the house was still very much alive, brooding, growing, waiting for new occupants to feast upon.

Before I present to you – and encourage you to study – possible explanations on what may be behind these events, we must first understand my own experience at the house. For those not familiar with *A most haunted house,* I present it now in its original format. For those that have already delved into the account, you now can relive the experience with new information, new insights, and I am also confident you will look upon it with new eyes, develop new theories and conclusions on what you believe is happening there.

I am not going to change the original documentation as I have established it was my testimonial and why I hid behind a veil of anonymity to protect vulnerable aspects of my life which I felt were open to attack. I hope you appreciate my reasons for that.

I have written *A most haunted house* as two personalities. One as the investigator trying to make sense of it all a decade later, an investigator trying to distance himself from his vulnerability, to attempt to gain control of his life and the events that occurred there. The second personality, John, was my attempt to reach catharsis, the baring of my soul, warts and all, of my experience to help understand what I had been through. The details from the other people are as accurate as possible given it is based on conversations that took place in 2003 and in early 2004, as well as a few participants allowing me to record their retrospective commentaries in 2012. The events documented and presented occurred over three months in 2003.

A most haunted house is a very different account from that of Dai and Anne. The style is the same but the experiences different. Was my experience different due to the short amount of time I lived there? Was it because of how my brain perceived the world? Was I already a soft target? Were there cracks already in the blossoming relationship ready to be preyed upon? Had the entity that dwelled there changed, evolved? Regardless it was a terrible time and sadly not the happy ending that Dai and Anne experienced. You will, of course, observe the connections that couple their account with mine.

As concerning it, presenting both testimonials together will give you a better understanding of the house and the experiences that reside within, and again as a collective we can try and make sense of something truly unrecognisable. Once again, we revisit that house in Haverfordwest. Here in its complete format as edited by GV Thomas is *A most haunted house*.

A most haunted house

By GL Davies

The house first came to my attention a few years ago. I'd heard rumours of a prolific paranormal case that exhibited all the aspects of a good haunting. It's always difficult when studying possible paranormal incidents to decipher fact from fiction and to explore the truth behind such talk. As always, first dismiss rational explanations for the events. A bird's nest in the attic and an overactive imagination can suddenly become a very real and frightening paranormal experience. Only when a thorough investigation has taken place can an assessment be made. Often investigators in this field tend to be too open-minded, and fall foul of the power of suggestion and a desperation to prove that these things do exist. Whilst others are so sceptical that even if there were proof of a paranormal phenomenon they would simply dismiss the notion. It's all about balance and working through a series of processes. Eliminating the options until eventually you are left with (hopefully) either an explanation or an event. Nine times out of ten it is something simple and mundane, but there are those rare cases when rational thought and science cannot explain what is happening.

One element of the story that did capture my imagination was that the house and the people that lived there wanted to remain anonymous. Either this was nothing more than a spooky story with no substance, or something had been happening to the people and they wished it to remain private for fear of ridicule. In my experience, people don't wish for real incidents of paranormal phenomena to be made public. They have to live and deal with what can be very confusing and frightening phenomena. People have approached me in the past claiming spectral, poltergeist or even alien activity. In reality, they craved attention and wanted to have the sense that something special was happening to them. Consciously or not, they were desperate for their existence to have more meaning and feel they had been chosen or selected by a higher unknown force.

A source gave me the general location of the property, and to my surprise I found it not to be some gothic or ancient-looking building, but a stereotypical street of terraced houses in Pembrokeshire in the centre of Haverfordwest. The area being mere minutes' walk from local supermarkets, schools, shopping centre and amenities.

Haverfordwest serves as the market town for most of the county of Pembrokeshire, West Wales. It forms an important hub between other towns in Pembrokeshire such as Milford Haven, Pembroke Dock, Fishguard and St David's as a result of its position at the tidal limit of the Western Cleddau river. The majority of the town, comprising the old parishes of St Mary, St Martin and St Thomas, lies on the (west) bank of the river, whilst on the left bank are the suburbs of Prendergast and Cartlett. At this point, a pair of sandstone ridges extending east-west and separated by a deep, narrow valley are cut through by the Western Cleddau. This leaves two high spurs on the west side of the river. On the northern spur, the castle and its surrounding settlement form the core of St Martin's parish. On the southern spur, the High Street ascends steeply from the river and forms the core of St Mary's parish. From the foot of each spur, ancient bridges cross the river to Prendergast: St Martin's Bridge ("the Old Bridge") and St Mary's Bridge ("the New Bridge", built in 1835). St Thomas' parish occupies the south side of the southern spur. From these core areas, the town has spread, mainly along the ridges. In addition to the four ancient parish churches, the remains of an Augustinian priory are visible at the southern edge of the town.

Haverfordwest has a deep and rich history of folklore and hauntings and even numerous UFO sightings during the 1970s that led to the area becoming known as the Welsh Triangle.

Some investigating led me to believe that I had found the exact location of the house in which this haunting was said to have occurred. I was excited but deeply anxious on how to approach the persons involved. I did not wish to seem overly presumptuous or assertive, or to be viewed as obnoxious or to be deemed insensitive. I decided to simply write a letter, explain who I was and my background as an investigator. I explained that if they did have a possible haunting, I would very much like to investigate it. I assured them that I would at all times respect their anonymity, and may perhaps be able to offer a solution or help them make sense of what was happening.

Two weeks went by and I had decided that perhaps I had been misled or had mistaken the property for the one in the story. If that was the case, further research was needed to either confirm such a house did exist or to simply close the file as just an example of hearsay or urban myth. Then I received the email.

It was from a gentleman who had lived there at the alleged time of the incidents. He had been forwarded the letter, had mulled over the notion of an outsider wishing to scrutinise a very private matter and had needed to speak to the other people connected. He politely informed me that those involved did not and would not speak to me, and to never make any contact with the residents of the house nor to mention his name. I replied, profusely apologising, saying that my intent was of a scientific and investigative perspective rather than one of glorification or an attempt to exploit the people affected.

Had someone else been barking up this tree? Had others called in the name of paranormal study or with claims of abilities to help stop the antics of something intangible to science? Was the rumour of this haunting malicious, created for some malevolent reason perhaps during some personal feud? Or maybe, just maybe, there was some substance to this. As compelled as I was to pursue this further, I had to respect the man's wishes.

Dispirited, I closed the case and moved on.

With Pembrokeshire's rich tapestry of paranormal stories interwoven into the fabric of its history, I was soon busy again investigating and generally enjoying the subject in the beautiful county. But, like a seed starting to germinate, the house in Haverfordwest grew and grew in my mind. Soon it was eclipsing my everyday thought and haunting my dreams. I had cerebrally connected to the house in a way I could not understand. I was tempted to walk by it but rationale and resolve told me to stay away, to respect the people's wishes and not be discouraged by the failure to study the case in depth. I decided I needed a break and booked a flight to Ireland to visit an old girlfriend.

After two days of relaxing, I checked my emails to discover, rather unexpectedly, a message from the man from the house. My first presumption was that perhaps someone had told him I was still pursuing the case and that had agitated him. Surprisingly, he said that all involved had decided to talk to me about the house on the prerequisite that they were to remain anonymous and that the location of the house never be revealed. I was to take no photos inside or outside of the house and that arrangements would be made for me to speak to everyone involved so that concurrent and thorough documenting could take place. They hoped that it would be a cathartic experience and it may begin to make sense to them if explained to an outsider, particularly one with experience of the subject. They hoped there was an answer. I knew now that something was indeed happening in the house. I was delighted beyond belief, but at the same time, there nagged a dark foreboding about the house and it burrowed deep within my mind.

Two weeks later, the interviews had been completed and I have arranged these into a chronological order of events. The names of the people have obviously been changed along with any key information that may link the house and the people involved. Those I spoke to have nothing to gain from this recounting and there was genuine emotion and a sense of dread, fear and confusion and if what did happen there is true then this is truly one of the most disturbing and prolific hauntings investigated.

I shall leave you, the reader, to decide and draw your own conclusions.

John and Sarah are the principal witnesses to the events that occurred. I met John at a coffee shop by the River Cleddau in Haverfordwest for his interview over a period of two days. At a later date, I met Sarah at her home a few miles away. All names in this transcript have been changed to protect the identities of the people involved. Neither currently live at the address. I also had the opportunity to speak to other relevant people who were witness to occurrences and events which have been included. I have edited the conversations into a more flowing fashion for the reader. Everyone involved has given me their consent for the publication of the events, for which I am grateful. Here are the testimonials and I gladly extend the opportunity to the reader to decide for yourself, based on your own personal views and through the evidence presented to create your own theory on the case.

John: I met Sarah through work. It was one of those incidents where we both clicked straight away. This was about ten years ago, so I was in my late twenties and she was a little younger. Everyone would tease us about getting together but the timing was always wrong. She left and came back a year later and we both hit it off again and started dating.

Sarah: John was different back then, always laughing and joking, always kind and friendly and was always so confident. I liked him so much. I was very attracted to him, but I guess we didn't want to ruin a good thing but yeah... we got together eventually and it was great. It was a good time in my life. Wow, it seems so long ago now.

John: After a few months, we got a little flat together in the town centre a few minutes' walk from the shops. It was a nice time. We had no TV, and would drink wine and chat and smoke and listen to music. The flat always seemed so bright and airy in hindsight. It sounds berserk now, but it was almost as if it was blessed.

Sarah: John loved that old flat so much; he could see the castle from the window. He loved popping down to the bakery to get fresh bread, or get the paper or coming home with a few bottles of wine. People would visit all the time. It was nice as we were literally in the town centre so our friends and family would pop over on a Saturday on their way through town and we would have friends over in the evenings for supper. It felt good, it felt grown-up, maybe a little pretentious with the music and wine and no TV but at that time we were happy with each other and we didn't need anything else.

John: Not to say it was perfect as we did have rows as every couple does. Couples who say they don't argue will one day have a huge row and that's when things go wrong, quickly. My advice is to not let things fester. It was a good time, I never wanted to leave, but I guess we were heading towards thirty and it was a one-bedroom flat. I think Sarah might have started thinking about having a family and settling down, not paying rent and working and paying towards something that was ours, but if there was a time machine then I would jump in it and travel back to 1st August 2003 and make sure that day played out differently. I will never forget that date, never, and I never wanted to leave. But a relationship is about two people not just one. You think that your doubts are just manifested through fear of the unknown, or because you don't like the idea of being tied down to a massive responsibility. It was never because I did not want to live and spend my whole life with Sarah. That was never the case.

Sarah: We were in work together and I was reading the local paper, the *Western Telegraph*, and I saw the house up for sale and I couldn't believe it. Some friends of mine had lived there for a bit and I had stayed over after a night out. I remembered it being a cool place and I thought I'd love a place like this one day. It had so much character. So many houses have the same set-up, this was different. It was lovely.

John: I was sat in the office when Sarah came in with a great big smile and a copy of the paper under her arm. She showed me the house, a little black and white advert of a terraced house that I had walked past a million times and never even noticed. I have to admit that I didn't like it. I didn't want to go from the flat and rush into anything. I guess my lack of enthusiasm was painted on my face as her smile just vanished and she looked really hurt. I remember we had a huge bust-up.

Sarah: We had a discussion on the future and where we were going. I could not believe why he wasn't more excited. Even to just go and look at it. I knew if he just looked at it then he would love it.

John: Sarah was furious when I said that we should have some kind of prenuptial. I think we had been together close to a year and surely that's not long enough. I laugh now but I had seen so many of my friends and family lose homes and end up with nothing. That sounds terrible right? It's like I was thinking the worst before it even happened but realistically everyone likes to think it through… yeah? Anyway I felt bad about it and told her to book us a viewing. As I said, if I could travel back in time I would have said no. I know we would have been at odds, maybe even had a huge falling out but we would have worked through it. I loved her so much. She was so beautiful and smart and I think that love was what made me say yes to view the house. What was the worst that could happen, right?

Sarah: I did feel a little selfish but I knew it would be for the best and we were paying something near £350 to £400 a month for a small-town flat plus bills on top of that. Also we could have no pets apart from a hamster, there was no garden and guests had to sleep on a bed settee in the living room, plus we were only a little bit further away. It was no difference in the time it took us to get to work or to go to the shops. John sulked for a bit but men do have a tendency to do that anyway when they don't get their way. I felt that we were basically wasting money renting and at the time it felt right for us to take that next big step, to commit to each other and really start thinking about our future. It feels so strange saying that now.

John: To be honest, I didn't know much about buying a house, all I knew was that it was hard work and took a long time. In my mind we would view it and not be able to afford it or someone else would gazump it. Gazump, that is a word, right? The house was valued at something crazy like £125K and I thought on our wages combined we could not afford that. But Sarah was the smart one, always was and always will be. She had done her research and even before the viewing of the house, in her mind it was ours. She came in on the 1st to tell me and the viewing was on the 3rd! I was livid, I was hoping it would take longer. So off we went from work one evening to see this place.

Sarah: I remember being so excited, and it was a beautiful evening and the sun was shining. We got to the house and I squeezed John's hand so hard. I knew, I just knew he would love it. I had had a call from the estate agent a few hours before to say that they couldn't make it, but the woman who owned the house was happy to show us around.

John: It looked nothing special on the outside. There are a hundred or more houses in Haverfordwest that look the same. It was quite near a main road and I liked the fact that our flat was down a little lane out of the way but still in the centre of town. Sarah knocked on the front door, and this woman, sullen and joyless, probably a bit older than us answered. She didn't seem that excited that we were there. In my mind she would have been baking bread, tidying and arranging flowers around the house to make it more homely. In hindsight I bet she thought we were just another dumb young couple, looking to play grown-ups and there was no way she was going to get us to buy so she could get out of the house with a profit. It was like she was just going through the motions. She made absolutely no effort in her appearance or making the house look nice and tidy. I'm not a snob, but seriously? Make an effort. Also it seemed a bit weird that even the estate agent didn't turn up. I just thought they were probably enjoying a pint in a beer garden somewhere like maybe we should have been doing. At the time you don't notice things like that, but I just thought the woman who owned the house was a bit of a weirdo.

Sarah: I have to admit the woman who owned the house didn't give us much of a welcome. It was like we were a nuisance. We went in and she said, "This is the living room, dining area over there; kitchen and bathroom back there and have a look upstairs." She explained the layout in about a minute and said to look around if we wanted. It was like the life had been sucked out of her. I thought maybe she worked nights or something.

John: I thought, wow! She's selling this so well, this woman should be on *The Apprentice*. This was a £125K investment to us, not a second-hand lawnmower. Her lack of enthusiasm made me want to just walk out.

Sarah: It was easy to sense that John was upset by the woman, but thankfully, I had been in the house before and I knew where everything was so I conducted the tour of the house.

John: She hadn't even tidied up but I'll admit, with the sun shining through the window, I was surprised by how long the house was. It looked tiny on the outside and stretched way back. I could see why Sarah liked it, it was like a TARDIS. However, that woman's attitude really pissed me off.

Sarah: I took John up the stairs to show him the three bedrooms.

John: The advert said three bedrooms. There were in fact two. There was a master bedroom, a strange shaped attic conversion and a box room so small that a cat would get claustrophobic.

Sarah: I didn't know that there was a child living with the woman and when we went up to the attic conversion she was lying on the wooden floor colouring in some pictures she'd drawn. She was only about seven and the first thing she asked was, "Are you going to buy this so we can find a new home?"

John: What a strange question, then it clicked. The mum had put the kid up to it as emotional blackmail! In hindsight I wish I had paid more attention to what the girl was drawing, as it was probably of me chained to the bed, with my head spinning and spewing pea soup or something. It was such a weird set-up. You don't prepare for these things but seriously, it was such a strange evening.

Sarah: I asked the woman what came with the house and she said the carpets and the kitchen furnishings. I asked her how low would she go in terms of the offer for the house and she said £105K. I was shocked as it was advertised at £125K, and she was happy to drop twenty thousand pounds. She quickly added that that was what she had paid for it.

John: I immediately thought, what was wrong with it? This was in good economic times, not like now with the credit crunch. And there was me thinking that someone would outbid us, or we would not be able to afford it and now the woman was desperate to get what she paid for it, not what it was valued as. Was there subsidence or damp or bad neighbours? There had to be something, but it seemed that woman and her kid just wanted to get out of there. I thought that maybe she and her husband had split up and she just wanted out. I don't think she was from around here. There are a lot of people down here in Pembrokeshire because of the military bases or oil refineries in the area.

Sarah: I took John into the garden, a lovely long garden with a shed at the end. We stood on the decking, I knew John would love the decking, and I just blurted, *"Let's do this. Let's go for it."* We could afford it on our wages. It was a bargain and it had a garden and spare rooms and it wouldn't work out much more than what we were paying for at the flat.

John: I admit that the place seemed really nice. I won't exaggerate and say that I sensed there was something wrong or that there was a feeling of foreboding. There was nothing like that at all, just a nice house. I said to Sarah that we need to think about it, need to talk first and work it out. I remember Sarah beaming like a kid who has been told they can have a present if they are good. As I said Sarah was smart and if we went for this then she would work out how we could do it. It was nice there on the decking with the sun shining. I love the summer and I can't abide the winter. I started imagining us living there, making plans for the decking, like we already lived there. That's always a mistake when you move in, imagining and creating in your mind. On the walk home Sarah was quiet; she was always quiet when she was computing in her mind. She was processing and organising everything that needed to be done; it's an amazing skill to have.

Sarah: John left everything to me, which was for the best. He of course came with me to the mortgage advisor and to the bank and to the estate agents. We put in an offer of £105K and it was accepted straightaway. I was so anxious that it would all go wrong and we would lose it but on 6th September 2003 we had the keys. It happened so fast, it was incredible.

John: You have to give all the credit to Sarah; she worked so hard to make sure everything was in order. I was of course sad to leave the flat, but once you started boxing things up and changing your details for the post, you kind of disconnect and look forward to the new place. I was excited, I just wanted to click my fingers and be there in the new house with all the furniture in place. Plus we could have Sky TV at our new place which was exciting and Sarah started talking about kittens and puppies.

Sarah: John was like a kid because we would have Sky TV. The night before we were to have friends and family help us move in, he went over and cleaned the empty house from top to bottom, everything!

John: I actually spent the first night there on my own, cleaning, tidying, and organising. My dad popped over with a bag of cleaning stuff and I showed him around. He loved the place; the house seemed much bigger as it was empty of furniture and clutter from the woman and her daughter. You came in through the front door into a tiny little hallway and then a door led you into the living room. In front of you was a big old fireplace with a window to your right. Off from the living room was a dining area with two doors, and under the stairs was a little alcove. One set of double doors took you to the kitchen and through patio doors to the decking area and garden. The other door led to the bathroom. The stairs had no railing and had a small landing. The doors up here were thick and heavy with black latches, quite old-fashioned but I liked them. One door opened to a small room which overlooked the street, another door to the main bedroom and finally the third to an attic conversion which was a low-ceilinged room with wooden floors. You couldn't stand straight, but it was long and quite wide and this part of the house due to its design was not attached to any of the other houses. Immediately I thought DEN! I could play music and not annoy the neighbours, drink wine, and play video games in this room. Sarah had designs on it to be a spare room, but we did compromise. The room was weird, like some do-it-yourself enthusiast had gone mad with little cupboards, nooks and crannies. There was a door to the boiler at one end and a little door as you came in that ran the length of the room and was filled with Christmas trees and decorations from previous occupiers. I have to say that I felt nothing untoward that night. I had the radio on and I thoroughly cleaned the place and scrubbed the decking too. Dawn came and the sun shone through the one window at the front of the house and I loved the place. Sarah was right. It was a good place at that time.

Sarah: We didn't have much to move and some good friends and family got vans to help us. It was fun, the bed belonged to the flat and we had a few bits and bobs but not a huge amount. Family gave us a dining table and we bought a fridge and found a second-hand washing machine that was advertised in the paper. We didn't even have a bed but John said, don't worry we will sleep in sleeping bags till it arrives and have fish and chips for our first official night. Both of us were eager to get unpacked. We just had to wait for a proper sofa and for the bed to be delivered.

John: First night was kind of romantic, snuggled up on the bedroom floor in our sleeping bags, big grins, madly in love. We had work the next day and I slept fine, not a peep in the night.

Sarah: First night was absolutely fine. My alarm goes off at 7 on the dot and John's literally a few seconds later. So I'm lying on the floor when my alarm goes off and then John's. He shuts it off and the door to the bedroom just opened. It swung open. I could have sworn it was on a latch and the carpet was thick so you had to push it. John laughed and said, *"OK, OK, we're getting up,"* like the house wanted us up.

John: The bedroom door opened on the first morning, just swung open. I said something like *"Someone's fed up with us after just one night."* I thought I heard the latch lift but I won't swear to that.

Sarah: To be honest I didn't think much about it after as we had to go to work. Everyone was excited about our move plus we still had lots to do with deliveries and unpacking. I had a lot of planning to do and of course a day's work too.

John: The door opening, I love stuff like that; well I used to love stuff like that. When I used to live back at my father's I liked all the shows about ghosts and I loved *The X-Files*. I loved it on Christmas Day when the family got together; someone would always have a ghost story.

I remember with the door that it opened a little bit at first, like someone was peeping through, and then it opened fully even on the thick carpet. In my mind it was like when I was little and my gran or dad would open the door a little to see if I was still asleep and when they saw me waking they would come on in. I miss my gran very much.

Sarah: I feel bad about this as I gave John hell, but I used to keep all the important documents for the house in a file in a draw. You know, all the mortgage details, bills and so on, and I kept everything organised. He didn't have to do much but sign where he had to sign. One day John and his mate were moving this big old heavy leather sofa, very old-fashioned, that we had bought from a second-hand furniture shop. I needed to send off documents and I couldn't find them in the draw. I checked where I thought they could be and thought, it's definitely in the house as I had them here yesterday.

John was struggling to get the sofa in and I ask him where are they, and he said he didn't know. I said, he must, as I didn't have them and they had been in the top draw. John and his mate get the sofa in, and he's sweating and flustered and says, *"Have you checked the top draw?"* Of course I bloody had and we had a row. It was the first time we had rowed in front of a friend before. He swore on his life that he had not touched them. We calmed down and I kept looking. I couldn't find them and had to go through all the hassle of getting them redone, so I got on my mobile and rang whomever it was I needed to get it sorted with.

John: She was adamant that I hid them from her. Why would I do that? I like a prank as much as anyone, but not with important stuff. However, I never doubted her, she was that organised, but moving house is stressful and maybe she had just forgotten where she had put them. I wasn't cross with her. It was just the settee weighed a ton and it was a nightmare to get into the house, and a joke that maybe the hamster had them did not help at all.

Sarah: I was so upset that they had gone missing but John said he would help me look and we would find them. To make matters worse, a few hours later, I decided I did not like where the settee was placed as I wanted it under the window. John and I pulled it across the room and John was staring at the floor. He looked so confused and there they were, the documents had been under the sofa. John swore they were not there when he put it down and I thought I would never leave something so important lying on the carpet with the front door wide open while they were getting the sofa in.

John: I couldn't explain it at all. I honestly did not see them when we brought in the settee and maybe I wasn't paying attention. My mate who was helping said he didn't see anything, but as I said maybe we just didn't pay any attention. Sarah went very quiet as either she doubted herself or she blamed me; it was a strange afternoon.

Sarah: We soon forgot and got on with making the house a home. I was looking in the paper one night and some kittens were free to a good home and it was only a few minutes' walk away. I told John and he was happy enough and we went and got a kitten.

John: I love animals but that kitten hated me. I got on better with the hamster. I even bought it a big climbing tree which it only used when I wasn't there! Anyway, I was sitting on the settee watching a DVD; we had a TV set but no Sky or anything yet. I think I was catching up on the series *24*. The kitchen doors were open and it was dark back there. I thought I heard a noise and presumed it was the kitten or the fridge making a noise.

As I looked away I thought I saw like a little surge of energy, a small ball of electricity. It was only for a second. I walked through the dining area into the kitchen. I didn't feel nervous or anxious. I thought maybe the cooker was playing up or it was a light from outside reflecting back in. The cooker was off and I went out the back on the decking and there was nothing unusual. I went back to the settee and it happened again. Now, I was worried as I suffer from migraines with what's called an aura. It's very common and they impair me so much that I have missed work and get-togethers with friends and family as I'm useless when they strike. I can't see, I can't talk, and I have numbness in my arm and then have a cracking headache over my eye. I'm not afraid to admit but sometimes the pain is so severe that I've cried. One of the symptoms I have affectionately called the worm; it's a light that impairs my vision, like a blue worm across my vision which makes it difficult to focus. It's the first symptom and I thought, *"Oh no, not a migraine!"* No migraine came so I just shrugged it off and never mentioned it to Sarah.

Sarah: One night I came out of the bathroom after a shower and John was taking pictures of the kitchen in the dark. I thought he'd gone mad, and he said that he thought the kitten was playing on its climbing tree in the kitchen and he wanted a photo. The kitten was upstairs sleeping on our bed. I just thought it was John being John. You know, he was kind of kooky.

John: A few nights later I saw the little light again, and this time I ran and got our camera and took a few pictures. I got them developed a few days later and there was nothing to see, just the flash on the patio doors and the kitchen and the cat's climbing tree. Sarah must have thought I'd had some kind of breakdown.

Sarah: I didn't feel that anything strange was happening and we started settling into a nice routine. We would finish work and John would have a bottle of wine open or a pot of green tea, and we had a TV now. We'd snuggle up on the sofa, I'd have the kitten all cwtched [*snuggled up*] up with me and we had just got into 24, the TV series.

John: We'd settle down for the evening and watch DVDs and I remember so vividly seeing something out of the corner of my eye towards the kitchen. We had this cream carpet and the light from the TV made everything look brighter, but around the kitchen and bathroom area was shadowy. I was very aware of something moving. At first I just thought it was the flickering of the TV casting shadows, playing with my mind. This blur would disappear into the shadows and be gone, but every night it came back. I could only see it from the corner of my eye and couldn't focus on it directly.

At one stage I was so sure that I saw it that I got up to look. Sarah asked what was I doing and I said I thought I had seen a rodent, a rat or something moving by the kitchen. That is how convinced I was. This happened for a week and I did not utter a word to Sarah after I said I thought I saw a rat, as I didn't want to upset her after everything with the bedroom door opening, the documents moving and the lights in the kitchen. Then one night this shadow, this blur moves up to the armchair we had across the room and it just stood there for a minute and disappeared back into the shadows. As I'm telling you now it has my hairs standing on end. It was a few feet tall and it seemed as if each day it got braver or stronger and got closer and closer. The night I knew something was happening and I hadn't gone mad was when it made its way in front of the TV and Sarah grabbed my arm.

Sarah: I had seen it for days, slowly moving by the kitchen and disappearing in the shadows. It was small, maybe two feet tall. It had no real form, just something in the corner of the eye, and the night it stood in front of the TV you could see it, a strange black blur. It is so strange to describe, you would have to see it to understand.

I squeezed John's arm so hard it bruised, and then the TV went black for a second and the thing was gone. That was the last time we saw the blur; it was moving around the room at floor level for around two weeks every night and then it made itself known and we never saw it again.

John: Sarah and I were really calm about it. We were of course a little frightened but as far as I knew we had a ghost. It was as simple as that. You hear so many stories of hauntings and pretty much everyone I know has a story about a ghost or a UFO. What can you do, call the police? Get a priest? This thing did not seem bad, I did not get a sense of dread, and it just spooked me. I thought it was cool at the time, maybe get some evidence, get a picture and make a fortune. But we decided not to tell anyone as people would be coming over to stay and visit, and we did not want to upset them. I thought, I'm not going to lose any sleep over it. It's mad to think that things got so bad that I began to dread the night, but I'm getting ahead of myself.

Sarah: I was upset, really upset. I didn't want to believe in such things. I told myself that there had to be an explanation. John loved it, I knew he did, but I hated it. My first thought was that maybe there was carbon monoxide in the room or something that was causing us to hallucinate. It was always at the same time of night, around 10pm, and both of us had seen it. John got mad when I made us watch TV with the light on.

I asked my dad to come over and he put in a brand-new carbon monoxide detector and checked the boiler and everything. He said it was fine but I still got the gas man to check. He said everything was in good working order. John started staying up later after I went to bed to watch DVDs but I knew he was down there with his camera trying to get a photo. I just wanted him to come to bed and snuggle, not be a ghostbuster. I was terrified on my own.

John: I have to say that it did excite me to the extent that I thought, if we could record evidence, we could be rich and famous! I know it sounds stupid now, but that's what I thought. It was my very own X-file! I was like the people on *Most Haunted*. Sarah thought it might be the boiler, or radon gas seeping through the floor, plus there was all this fuss about this new mobile phone technology that was going to be used in the area; leaflets came through the door saying that it needs to be stopped, petitions need to be signed and protests attended as the technology was based on Cold War weapons, made people depressed and ill, and could even cause diarrhoea. Berserk, I know, but it's a theory and who knows maybe it was responsible. The house was quiet too; the walls were so thick that you never heard the neighbours to either side of us: no TV, there were no arguments heard and not even a headboard banging in the night. The walls were stone and probably a few feet thick.

Sarah: Nothing seemed to happen for a few weeks and the nights began to draw in and the house seemed warm and comfortable. John, the kitten and the hamster all seemed settled. John hates the winter as he suffers from a seasonal disorder that makes him prone to depression. I didn't fully appreciate at the time what it is, but it's awful to see someone so bright and cheerful become more and more down and sorrowful, but he would always try and fight it. Well, he did but I guess he just got worn down by everything that started to happen.

John: The cat and I started to get on a bit, and it would chill out more and sit by me on the settee. The hamster would roll about in its big plastic ball on the carpet and they both got on well. One evening I walked from the kitchen into the dining room and there on the settee the cat was hissing at something, its ears back and tail snaking around. I thought, what's up? I said, "Lucky." Lucky was the cat's name. It just growled this insane growl, and I walked towards the settee and it was like I had walked into something absolutely freezing. We had radiators on, we had been cooking and Sarah had been in the bath so the house was warm and cosy.

I could literally map the area of the coldness with my hand; it was about four feet tall and maybe a foot across, and from the top to the carpet it was freezing. Then in a second it was back to normal temperature and the cat just scarpered upstairs. I have since read about cold spots, but it was like there was something there, just stood there, staring at the cat and the cat could see it, sense it. I don't know how to describe it but the cat was certainly aware of it.

Sarah: John told me about Lucky; but animals, particularly cats, always have a tendency to do that weird hissing and staring at the wall thing. I just thought the cold spot was a draft or maybe something to do with the fireplace. It was blocked up but maybe a brick had come loose. I wasn't there so I can't give any more information on that.

John: About this time we finally had our Sky installed. I was thrilled we could finally catch up on so much TV that we'd missed. The guy who installed it I knew well, as a friend of mine had married his sister, and he set the TV all up and showed me how it all worked; you couldn't fault the service. Sarah and I were excited. She'd just had her bath and we settled down and at 10pm it just went off. I was cross as you would expect, as we were excited. Next day I call Sky; they said there was no fault but they would try something or other. I get home from work and it's working fine. 10pm it goes off, I'm decidedly pissed off. So Sarah calls Sky in the morning, and they say there is no detectable fault from there but there was obviously a problem and they would send out an engineer.

The same guy who set it up comes over, and again he's great, he puts in a new box, does a load of tests, and checks the signal and all's fine. That night at 10pm off it goes. Three new boxes and a new dish later the problems are finally solved. We were told that they could not understand what was happening, that the signal and the equipment were working fine. I have had Sky before and after and never experienced anything like that. You start to think, *"Was that just a genuine fault or was something messing with us."*

Sarah: The problem with the satellite dish was so strange and the poor people on the phone and the engineer must have thought we were nutters because they couldn't find a problem. It did cause stress between us because at one time John just gave up and went straight to bed after we finished work. His SAD

[*Seasonal Affective Disorder*] was starting to kick in and he just wanted to relax and enjoy our evenings together. I went up to see him; he said to just leave him alone. He was never usually like that. It's sad to see someone with so much energy just lying there looking lifeless and miserable, but he would drink and that never made it better, so maybe he was to blame for it to begin with.

John: I do get down but I always try and buck up. I remember one night I made a terrible mistake of getting hammered on a bottle of red. In the night I had to get up to use the toilet which was downstairs. I always tried to be quiet as I didn't want to wake Sarah; plus we had started to lock the kitten in the kitchen with its bed, litter tray and climbing frame. The kitchen doors would not close tight so we rested a dining chair against the doors to stop Lucky from escaping and running around the house. The hamster was normally up at night doing hamster things in its cage but you get used to it. I put on the landing light which was enough for me to see down the stairs and the bathroom door. I tiptoed down, went in the bathroom, turned on the bathroom light and went to the loo.

I was stood there and this overwhelming coldness overtook me; all the hairs stood up on my neck and on my arms, and I swear I felt a breath on my neck. It was as if someone was stood right up close behind me. I was petrified, absolutely terrified and I spun around expecting to see Sarah, to see something. Nothing was there. I dashed off up the stairs and hid in bed with the landing light still on. That was the first of many times that would happen to me.

Sarah: Yeah, it happened to me lots. A few times when I got out of the shower I felt something there, just watching. Sometimes I would feel this deep coldness cover me. I know you're going to be cold when you get out of the shower but this was freezing cold. I would be sat on the loo and I could see my breath, that's how cold it would get. It was really unnatural. It got to the stage where I would try and be as quick as possible to have a shower or use the loo so as not to spend too much time in there. It was not a good feeling at all; I always felt a sense of menace.

John: There were times that I'd have a bath and Sarah a shower or vice versa at the same time as we did not like being in there alone at night. I can't recall very much happening in the daytime just mainly at night. This sounds very odd and people will think me mad, but I always, always got the sense it was a woman. I can't explain why I feel that, there was no perfume smell or anything to determine what it was, but from that first night, I always thought it was a woman.

Sarah: Funny that John would say that but I always sensed it was a man. It's strange how the imagination works but I imagined this creepy, leering man just lurking in there like some weirdo sex pest. We of course had double-glazed frosted glass with a curtain in there and there was a radiator that was on quite often airing our underwear or a towel. It was an awful thing to experience, you can't do anything. I cried one day, just by considering having a shower, as the feeling was so intense and so awful in there. People have no idea just how suffocating and harsh the atmosphere was in there. It was like a cold, sickly tension. But then, suddenly, it stopped for a bit, just long enough for us to think things were going to get back to normal. The house had a habit of doing that. It would do things and stop, just for a short time, and then it would do something new or something more intense.

John: All of this had taken place over about seven or eight weeks, because it really stepped it up a gear around the time the fair came to town, up in Portfield by the Rifleman's Field, which is normally the end of October, perhaps the start of November. When Sarah's twin nephews came to stay the weekend, we were to take them to the fair and they were going to see the kitten and our new place.

Sarah: I made John swear on his life that he wouldn't say anything or try and frighten the boys, but you could see in his eyes that the spark of excitement about the strange events had gone. It was no longer a ghost-hunting adventure to him. This was real and it was tiring and depressing. He looked drained and tired, and the winter was starting to entrench. He was drinking more, like he was just trying to knock himself out before bed and just get to the morning. I couldn't sleep. I'd hear the hamster in his cage, but now and again I thought I heard the bathroom door open and hear the stairs creaking. With everything going on, my imagination was running wild.

John: You know things have gone south when you're practically running to work in the morning to get some peace.

Sarah: My nephews, Eric and Sam, were coming over after school on the Friday. They were ten then and they were excited as we were going to the fair. John got on well with them both and we were both looking forward to having them over. I'd had this nagging feeling though, what if the house played up when they were here? What if they got scared or frightened? John thought that if they slept in the den then they should be OK as it was a new part of the house, an extension. Nothing seemed to happen in there are far as we knew. In fact John spent more and more time in there, watching DVDs and drinking wine. I felt like I was losing him.

John: I admit that the house was depressing me; the excitement was replaced with dread. I spoke to a few close friends about it and they suggested that we get the house blessed or call in a priest. Just sounds crazy now, something that science cannot prove exists affecting us so badly. I know this sounds stupid but I hated having a pee or going to the loo or having a shower because it was like there was something there; something wrong or sinister just watching.

Sarah: It practically ended any physicality between us, you know of an intimate nature. How could you be naked or physical while at the back of your mind you're anxious that something is watching or that something will open the door? Now and again we would stay at friends' and make up for it then. It was like a huge weight was lifted off our shoulders. It was new and like when we were together for the first time, but then we would also have this dread that we would have to go back to the house. What would be waiting for us? No home should ever feel like that.

John: It was good having Eric and Sam over, and it brightened the place up. They loved the cat and the hamster, and quickly made themselves at home. They loved playing on the PlayStation.

Sarah: We took them to the fair and it was nice to be out. I love the fair: the sounds of the generators, the smell of the candyfloss and hot dogs. The boys were running around, and John and I were trying to keep up. There was this really, really old-fashioned ghost train, well not so much a ghost train, but you walked in and went through some creepy rooms. I went in first with Sam and then John went in with Eric. Something happened because Eric came out on his own and said that John couldn't move.

John: I went in with one of the boys and it was a shitty ride that cost me £8 for four entries, just little rooms with lots of corners to walk around and mirrors and string hanging down so it felt like someone was touching your hair. Sam, no it was Eric, Eric thought it was rubbish, and darted off and came back saying it was dull and nothing happened. I kept expecting a man in a mask to dive out and frighten us. I got about halfway and there was a small room with a flashing light and I just freaked. I felt so despondent and low, like really depressed. I just felt like a statue. It sounds silly but I just wanted to be a kid again with my dad and gran. Life was so much easier then; back then, all this weird ghost crap was just stories and now it was real and in the home with me and the woman I loved. Maybe it was the nostalgia, memories of going to the fair with my father or the cold and dark of the winter, but I just had this mammoth feeling of despair.

Sarah: I had to go back on and spend another couple of pounds and get him out. He looked like he had been crying, but he came out and smiled and joked for the boys. He never let on but I felt like I had lost him that night. I felt like he regretted buying the house, that I had ruined him, ruined us. It was not my fault what was happening at the house. As we were mulling around the fair I met my friend who had owned the house prior, the time when I stayed over after a night out. Eric and Sam were on the bumper cars, and John and I had been waiting for them. We exchanged hugs and pleasantries, and John bluntly blurted, "Is the house haunted?" My friend paused and almost regretfully said it was. Her ex-partner who had lived there had had a rough time. She said that she was working nights and it got so bad that her boyfriend would sleep at his mum's house as he hated being there on his own.

John: Inside I was cross that her friend had never warned Sarah, but Sarah would not have listened anyway. Sarah was stubborn, and besides, who the fuck is going to believe that actual ghosts mess with people and haunt an actual house? I'm sorry for the language but it still frustrates me to this day. Anyway, she told us that her boyfriend, husband whoever he was, had seen things come down the stairs when he was sat watching TV. She claimed that it would walk around downstairs moving things, making noises, running up the stairs while he lay in bed terrified. It got to the stage that he had to go to his mum's just to sleep. I felt sick. I felt angry.

Sarah: She told us that one night her boyfriend called her, pleading for her to finish work early as he was frightened. Things had been happening in the house. She claimed she never saw anything; but that you knew there was something not right there. As she worked nights and was out on the weekends she didn't have much involvement, especially at night when the occurrences seemed stronger and more prolonged. I knew that their relationship ended suddenly and they sold up. Eric and Sam came off the ride and we quickly changed the subject.

John: We got home and I got straight on the wine. I was shaking. I kept getting chills up and down my spine and I knew that I was just freaking myself out. Every noise had to be a ghost, every creak was a ghost. I was losing it, I felt that it was pushing us out, constantly pushing our buttons. It was winning.

Sarah: I put the boys to bed and they were exhausted. I went downstairs and sat at the dining table was John with a massive glass of red wine. I sat by him and I told him off. I told him he had to get a grip, that whatever was happening had a rational explanation and the house was ours. Ours! I said that his SAD and his drinking were making him depressed and susceptible to anxiety and fear, and that we needed to be strong. To fight for our home by ignoring anything that was happening, to push back and be happy and embrace that happiness.

John: Sarah gave me a pep talk and you know what? She was right. At first I resisted all hope, and then I realised she was right. Maybe what was happening had an explanation, and if it didn't then push it out the way. We were alive and it was OUR home. A home where hopefully one day we would have children of our own and a life. I have to say that I felt better. We went to bed together that night and for the first time in a long time we snuggled and we slept well. It makes me sad now thinking of how happy we were for that brief time. It might have been the last time we were truly happy and in love.

Sarah: I woke up and the sun was streaming through the skylight and John was stretched out across the bed like a starfish and deep in sleep. I heard something shuffling around on the landing and the latch went on the door and it opened a little, but this time it was Sam. He looked tired and upset. I sat up and asked was he OK? He said that someone has been in the den with them opening the cupboard doors and running around. He said it wasn't very funny of John to play tricks like that.

John: I was so confused. I had slept all night. I slept in the inside of the bed against the wall as Sarah would get up first to use the bathroom. Sarah looked at me and she knew I hadn't moved but what do you say to the kid. "It's OK, son, it was a ghost," or "Yeah it was me sneaking around in a room with two ten-year-old boys sleeping in it." Either way it was going to portray me in a very poor light. I was furious, I knew what it was.

Sarah: I told Sam that it was probably the pipes or the neighbours in another house. I had no idea what to say so I just lied to him.

I was fortunate enough to have a telephone conversation with Sam [*real name changed to protect identity*] who, now 20 years old, had the opportunity to speak to his aunty Sarah about the night in question when he was much older. Eric his twin brother was unavailable for comment as he was currently working overseas. This is Sam's account and perspective on the events of that night:

Sam: What a strange night. I never really believed in ghosts and aliens but that night still gives me the shivers even now. I was only ten or eleven but I remember the night. Sarah and John had just bought this new house and they had got a cat, and it was around the time the fair was in town. We enjoyed seeing them as they were always fun and treated us like grown-ups and gave us more freedom to relax. We went to the fair and had a great time. I felt a little ill from the hot dogs and sweet stuff, but apart from that it was fun.

They had this strange attic conversion, a weird shape, low ceiling and everything made of wood. There was a fold-out bed in there and Eric and I shared it. It was cool in there as John had a PlayStation 2. We played some fighting game until Sarah popped her head in and said, "Time to sleep, boys." She left the landing light on, so light was coming in from under the door so you could make out the shape of the room, and we knew where to head to if we needed to get up in the night. At the far end of the room was a small door which was access to the boiler. You could hear the boiler doing its thing when John and Sarah were using the water or something downstairs.

I didn't feel uncomfortable at all, just tired and excited as in the morning we were all going to go into town for breakfast. I woke up and had no idea what time it was but the den was pitch black and no light was coming in under the door. I heard no boiler or anything but I heard what sounded like a door slowly opening. The sound wasn't coming from the direction of the main door, but the little boiler door at the other end of the den. Eric was fast asleep and breathing deeply. It sounded like the door opened and closed a few times, like it was opened as far as it could and then slowly closed again and then opened and so on, a few times. I was scared. I remember holding my breath trying to listen and then I heard what sounded like something run across the den, like tiny feet, not like an animal but like the way a child or toddler would. I was terrified but I was too scared to scream or shout. The footsteps ran straight past the fold-out bed and I heard what sounded like the whoosh, whoosh of material and then the boiler room door closed, not loudly with a bang but with more force than when I first heard it and it clicked as it closed shut.

Eric said he heard nothing or hadn't seen anything and I must have dreamt it, but I don't believe I did and it scared me. I hoped it was John playing a prank but Sarah told me in the morning that it was pipes under the floorboards, making it sound like someone was walking about and I believed her. It wasn't until a few years ago that she told me what had happened in the house. I think we were lucky, as scary as it was. Some of the stuff that happened would have put me in a mental hospital if I'd been there. I never stayed there again. I feel sorry for John, he was good to us and that was one of the last times we saw him. That house did, in my opinion, ruin them both. People can say it was a dream or I made it up, but it was real and frightening.

Sarah: When Sam was about 16, I had a chat with him about the house, the pressures it put on me and John. Sam was adamant that there was something in the room that night. Nothing could fit in the boiler cupboard as it was obviously filled with the boiler. You could say it was the wind or the pipes or even an animal on the roof or guttering; but I know that it was whatever inhabited the house with us. John initially joked in the early days that he didn't mind having a ghost as long as it helped towards the bills and he would blame odd socks on it, but by this stage it felt like we were being forced out, that we were the intruders.

John: After the night with the boys in the room I decided that I had to find out why this was happening. It wasn't a case of imagination or creaking old floorboards or the wind. There was something definite happening in the house. Not only had Sarah and I witnessed the activity, but it was of course affecting us, traumatising us. Now it was Sam who'd had an experience when he stayed over. Sarah's friend who had lived here had said that there was something not right with the place. I was beginning to feel like her ex must have. I took it upon myself to conduct some proper investigation. I even agreed to have the house blessed.

Sarah: Some friends of ours were into spiritual and holistic practice and they seemed very grounded and knowledgeable about spirituality and life after death. I spoke to one of them and they referred us to this middle-aged woman with a really nice demeanour. She was relaxed and said not to worry as she has experienced such things before and all the house needed was to be blessed and the spirits as she called them would find peace and leave and it would be like our home was new, and more importantly it would be ours again.

John: I started investigating where we lived and what used to be there before us but there was nothing of consequence that could be linked to a haunting, you know like an old hospital or a burial ground. Haverfordwest is a very old town and maybe something had been there. However, nothing leapt out at me in the research. I needed to find something that I could connect the hauntings to. The house had been built over a hundred years ago, and looking through the archives at the library I could not find anything about the address or the street. One very strange thing I discovered in the deeds was that seven different owners occupied that house since 1986. We moved there in 2003, so that's eight in less than twenty years. Maybe that was usual for the type of house and the worth and value of it, but in my mind I just thought about how sullen and odd the woman was who showed us the house on the viewing. Had she like us and Sarah's friend experienced strange and unusual behaviour in the house? It all started to piece together like a jigsaw, the eight occupiers in seventeen years, Sarah's friend's ex-partner and the sullen woman and her kid. There was something very wrong happening here and it wasn't only us that it had happened to.

Sarah: The spiritualist woman came over to the house one Saturday when John and I were at home. As soon as she came through the door she said, *"Yes, yes, there is something here."* She smiled and said that we shouldn't worry and that the house still had occupants from the past that either didn't want to go, or didn't know they had passed on.

John: What the woman said just chilled me. I was still sceptical, as we had told our friends what was happening and they had told this woman. She then had long discussions with Sarah on the situation. To be honest, it wasn't like she was there to see our new washing machine; she was there to help us get rid of the ghost or ghosts. She knew our predicament.

Sarah: It was a very relaxing experience. We sat in the living area and had a chat while drinking herbal tea. We talked about how it was affecting us as a couple and how what was supposed to be a good thing, buying and living in this house, for us was now a living nightmare. She spoke in depth that we had to emit an internal positive energy to push away the darkness and the sadness. She told us that our internal light would protect us from evil and be a beacon, to help the spirits pass into the spirit world and find happiness.

She lit some incense sticks around the room and then asked us to follow her as she walked around with a lit incense stick, making sure the smoke and fragrance went into every corner and into every room. She spoke softly, reassuring the spirits that everything would be OK in the spirit realm if they just let go. That it was mine and John's time in the house now and the house had to be a happy place, not a sad place for the dead to linger in. She said that the den had a vortex that was generating energy for spirits to manifest and she told them that their loved ones who had passed were waiting for them in the afterlife. It was very emotional and I felt tingles on my scalp, on down my neck and back. It was an amazing experience.

John: I expected the woman to say, *"This house is cleansed,"* like in the movie *Poltergeist* but I will admit I hung on to every word and I believed everything she said. I wanted a normal life together with Sarah and if this worked then great. I imagined that a bright orb of white light was in my chest pushing away the bad presence in the house.

Sarah: The woman left, and John and I hugged and I started crying. I so wanted this to work; we needed this to work.

John: Immediately after the house had been blessed we felt bright and cheery and nothing seemed to happen. The walls didn't start bleeding and the settee didn't start flying around the room. We were cautious of course, and still very worried, but I still believed in my bright orb light inside me and that the spirits had got to go to Heaven or wherever you go at the end. Then, it started again and this time it was more intense. It was much more frightening.

Sarah: I couldn't believe it. I just could not believe it. This time it felt like it was stronger, like it was angry that we dared try and evict it from its home. It was our home!

John: When it all started to kick off again I told Sarah to phone this spirit woman, but the woman said that she had tried and that the spirits obviously didn't want to go, and to try and get an exorcist! I was furious but Sarah said that the lady had tried to help us for free and that we had to be positive and keep believing that the house was ours and hopefully the spirits would give up and we would win.

The lady in question who performed the blessing was unavailable for comment.

John: The next few days, after the blessing, just going to the toilet or for a shower was depressing as the intensity of the presence in there was overwhelming. People say it's the living not the dead we need to fear but the psychological suffering was beyond belief. This sounds insane but I made sure I went to the toilet as much as I could in work so I didn't have to go at home. My thoughts were severely dark; I thought about death most of the time. I know I suffer with depression but never like that before. It was like hope finally died.

Sarah: One night I was in bed, John was back on the wine big time and was passed out next to me, snoring. I lay there in the darkness thinking, what had we done to deserve this and would things ever get better. I thought I heard a noise downstairs. I thought, please be the hamster running in its wheel or trying to gnaw its way through the cage again. So I'm lying there, trying to listen but John is snoring, so I try and nudge him so he turns on his side and he goes quiet for a bit, and then unmistakably, I hear the bathroom door open and close again. I just kept thinking over and over, "Please go away, please go away," then something ran up the stairs. In a few seconds, something made it up the stairs and on to the landing. It was so quick and I could sense that it was on the other side of the door and I swear I heard the latch jiggle, and then I screamed.

John: I don't know what happened but Sarah was screaming.

I woke up not knowing where I was or what was happening; I was still pissed. I jumped to the end of the bed and tumbled to the floor and Sarah turned on the light; she was sobbing uncontrollably. I asked what was happening and she said it was at the bedroom door. I tell you now, the last thing I wanted to do was to open that bloody door but I had to, just had to. So I pull up the latch slowly and pulled the door open. I expected to see a ghostly face or hell knows what and there was nothing. The landing was freezing cold and I was terrified. I thought, let's just pack our things and be gone.

Sarah: When John opened the door I just expected to see something there. Like a ghastly skulled ghoul or something from a horror movie; there was nothing. John said perhaps with everything that was going on that maybe I'd just had a nightmare but I was wide awake. I didn't drop off or get any sleep that night. I swear that something opened the bathroom door, closed it and then ran up the stairs and tried to open our bedroom door.

John: I don't think people will fully understand the intensity of it all. We had been in the house maybe ten weeks, maybe three months tops and all of this is happening. We'd gone from things going missing, to cold spots, lights in the kitchen, blurry little figures in the living room, the presence in the bathroom, Sam being upset in the den and now something running around in the dark while we were in bed. What a terrible, terrible time.

Sarah: A night or two later, and John and I are in the kitchen talking. We still had a life, you know, work, family and friends. Some friends were down the following weekend and they were going to stay at ours, we were planning for that, but all the time you're thinking: "Should we tell them, should we actually tell them that all this weird shit is going to happen?" But at the same time, you feel selfish. I didn't want to warn them as I needed them. I needed them to be in the house. John was drunk most evenings now and depressed, and our relationship was not in a good state. We were both scared and maybe if some other adults were in the house maybe we would be safer, maybe nothing would happen or if they experienced something then maybe they would have a solution or an explanation. I just wanted them to stay so badly.

John: I remember we were in the kitchen chatting and making supper when we heard above us footsteps. Now the den ran the length of the kitchen and above the bathroom and a little bit into the dining area. We hear these footsteps. They were heavy on the wood, not like a child as Sam heard but footsteps like lady's heels on the wooden floor, and they walked the entire length of the den. We looked at the ceiling like we were watching it happen, following it with our eyes and whatever was making those sounds turned on its heel and walked back across to above us and then we heard the boiler room door slam.

Sarah: It was so scary but John did the strangest thing. He ran and grabbed his camera and sprinted up the stairs and barged into the den and shouted, "Come on, you fucker, come on show yourself," while taking pictures around the den. The fact he took control made me feel better, but I just wish he hadn't baited it so much. We were to pay for that.

John: I guess I just lost the plot. I was sick and tired of its games. It had our attention and I wanted proof, hard proof that it existed so maybe I could take that evidence to someone who could help us or make us enough money so we could leave. I thought if this thing wants to frighten us then carry on and I'll catch it. I will get a photo or a recording and I would win, not it, but me. It was crazy to think that, but it's not like you have been burgled and you can fit better locks and get an alarm or a big dog. It's not like you're fighting a real person where you can kick or throw a fist or grab a baseball bat or scream for the police. How do you take on something there is no proof even exists? But guess what it goes and does next?

Sarah: As soon as John comes back into the kitchen the footsteps start again from above and he ran back upstairs and again nothing was there. It stopped as soon as he got to the top of the stairs. It was like it was playing with John or showing him who was boss. We got the photos developed the next day and there was absolutely nothing just the den illuminated by the flash. No ghostly apparition or orbs of light or strange shadowy figures. There was nothing.

John: I think it was the next night that was the worst night; it was horrible.

Sarah: What happened that night was terrifying. I don't expect people to believe what happened, and in fact I don't expect anyone to believe any of it. If you were not there or if you haven't experienced anything like it then how can you believe it?

John: We had gone to bed; I probably had been drinking, as I pretty much did every night. I dozed off and a huge crash woke me up. I thought maybe a car had crashed outside or someone had put a brick through the living room window.

Sarah: There was this smash, like a window being smashed in. I thought we were being burgled.

John: There was all this banging downstairs like the living room was being turned upside down. You could hear the draws being opened and slammed and you could hear rummaging. We were being burgled. All of this is happening so quickly. And then it sounded like someone ran up the stairs and we both heard the bedroom door being pushed. We heard the metal of the latch and then silence.

Sarah: It was like a few men were searching for something downstairs, opening cupboards, doors and draws, and then they came up the stairs and the door moved against the latch. I was paralysed with fear. You hear about robbers tying people up, hurting them, and doing much worse things. John got the light on and was sat there bolt upright with a mug in his hand like he was ready to throw it. I thought the police will be here on their way as someone must have heard the window smash and all the chaos downstairs. From the smash waking us up to the bedroom door being pushed took about thirty seconds. I was too frightened to even get up and dash across and get my mobile, which was charging on the dresser across the room.

John: Even with everything that had been happening nothing had scared me more than this, but you get these thoughts in your head like if there is someone in the house then I will hurt them. I will do what it takes to protect Sarah and us. I'm not a hard, tough bloke who fights or anything but at that moment I thought if someone is in the house and I hurt them or worse, then I would happily go to prison than see either of us get hurt. I would imagine any man out there who hears this would do the same. There was silence for ages, not a sound, and I had the lyrics of a song that I liked going around and around in my head, stuck in there like it was on repeat and it was from a band called System of a Down and the lyrics were: "I'm sitting in my room, with a needle in my hand, just waiting for the tomb, of some old dying man." People will laugh when they hear that, but I couldn't get those lyrics out of my head. Strange I know but I remember it so clearly, so vividly. I don't think it had any relevance to what was happening but it was just stuck in my mind.

Sarah: John whispered that it sounded like it was over, but I didn't hear anything go back down the stairs. I felt like something was still there on the landing maybe listening, trying to hear if we were awake or asleep. John started to get out of bed really slow with the mug in his hand. He was only in his boxers and he started to head for the dresser where our mobiles were. There were things like a brush, scissors, anything he could use as a weapon and then suddenly huge heavy footsteps ran down the stairs, then there was a huge crash and the slam of a door. It was awful, absolutely awful.

John: I thought that whoever was on the landing saw that we had the light on; heard me moving about, thought that we had no doubt called the police and got out of there as quickly as possible.

Sarah: John made for the bedroom door. I screeched at him, "What if they were still in the house?" He pointed at the skylight and whispered that the sun was starting to come up. He grabbed the scissors from the dresser and tossed me my phone which was dead despite me having it on charge all night. I was so frustrated and frightened.

John: I slowly opened the door – and fair dues to Sarah – she got out of bed and stood by me. I know it doesn't sound manly at all but I was glad she was with me. I slowly opened the door expecting a black-gloved hand to grab me but I could see nothing in the gloom. I flicked the landing light on and shouted as loud as I could, *"POLICE ARE ON THE WAY, HAND ME THE CRICKET BAT AND CALL YOUR BROTHERS!"*

Sarah: John shouted down the stairs, saying that the police were on the way and that we had weapons and people were on their way to help us. He did it so if there was anyone down there that hopefully they would panic and get out of there. We had nothing of worth, nothing of value, just a TV and DVD player, but nothing worth taking. You have to realise that we were pretty broke most of the time as we had to buy furniture and bits and bobs for the house; plus Christmas was around the corner and we never had much money in the house. Poor Lucky the cat was down there. I was worried he had escaped through an open door or smashed window or that they had stepped on him or done something terrible to him.

John: I was on the landing in only my pants and Sarah was holding on to my arm. I thought it had to be a smash and grab. There was only one window and door at the front of the house and near impossible to get in through the back garden. I didn't want to go down the stairs and I kept expecting to hear someone start shouting like the police or a neighbour to see if we were OK. I told Sarah to stay on the landing.

Sarah: John told me to stay. I didn't want to be alone but he said if someone was still downstairs then to run in the bedroom, and try and get the dresser in front of the bedroom door and try and get out through the skylight. I don't think I could have reached it or even fit through, it was only small, but I guess he was just trying to keep me safe.

John: I started going down the stairs. Dawn had broken but it was gloomy down there and I was bricking it. I kept expecting to see a man down there or for a hand to grab my foot on the way down. The bathroom door was wide open and the frosted window at the back was not smashed. As I came to the bottom of the stairs and into the dining area, I expected to see the window smashed behind the settee and the curtain billowing in the wind, but the window was fine. The kitchen doors were still shut with a dining chair against them to stop Lucky from running around at night. I flicked on the dining room and kitchen lights and there was no sign of a break-in. I turned on the light in the living room and opened the door to the little hallway that led to the front door, and the front door was intact, locked and chained from the inside. The front window had not been forced.

Sarah: I kept shouting, *"John, are you OK?"* And, *"John, what's happening?"* and he kept telling me to shush. Then he said to come down and that nothing had been broken into. He kept repeating, *"I don't understand, I don't understand."*

John: I told Sarah that it was OK to come down. As I turned, I saw over by the armchair the wooden unit thing where we kept our CD player and where Sarah had photos and things she collected. On the floor nearby were about a dozen or so CDs, and they had all been arranged into a spiral shape.

Sarah: When I saw the CDs all arranged into a spiral I just cried and sobbed and ran over and kicked them. John was mad saying we should have taken a picture as evidence. Evidence of what? Would people think that's definitely a ghost because it rearranged the CDs? No, they would think us insane. I remember just lying on the floor, sobbing. I had experienced the worst night of my life. I wanted to leave and never come back.

John: I think it would have been easier if we had been burgled as we could have dealt with that. We would have had the police over and fitted better locks and thought ourselves grateful that we were not harmed, but how do you deal with this? I swear to you now, it sounded like something tore that house apart and something ran upstairs and was stood on the landing pressed against the bedroom door. It must have happened around 6am and from the time I woke up to getting downstairs took about five minutes, tops. It was no hallucination or bad dream, it was no prank and Sarah and I were together in bed when we heard it. We both heard it, we both experienced it. Sceptical people out there can think what they want and I can't blame them, but something was in the house and it was mere feet from us behind the bedroom door. I held Sarah for ten, fifteen minutes while she sobbed and shook. She was in shock, we both were, and then she looked up and let out this massive wail.

Sarah: John was just holding me, telling me it would be OK. OK how? But he was trembling and he was crying too. I looked up at the kitchen door and there on the chair that was pushed against the kitchen door was a framed picture of us both. It was just leant against the back of the chair, facing us. I hadn't put it there, it had been on the wall, and I just screamed and screamed.

John: Whatever it was had sent us a powerful message. I just wanted to run out into the street and shout for help.

Sarah: You have no idea how it feels to be totally helpless. No one could help us. I knew we had to start to look for another place to live, but we had no money. Everything we had saved had gone into the house, and our friends and family had no room for us. I know they would want us, but you can't just move a home into someone else's. What could we do, go down to the council office and say, "Can we have a new house please, ours is haunted?"

John: I checked the rest of the house and there was definitely no sign of a break-in. The windows were locked from the inside and the front door still had the chain on. So there was, in my opinion, no way that someone had got into the house. Lucky was safe too. Sarah spoke to her dad who came over and I spoke to my best friend who did not know what to say. I knew it was no good calling these so-called ghost hunters, no offence meant, or a psychic medium. The woman who blessed the house had made it worse. We had to move out, but it's not like you can just get up and leave that instant. We needed to sell up or find someone to move in and rent it, and we needed money for temporary living. We both went to work that day and it was one of the longest days of my life.

Sarah: I just didn't want to go back at all, but on the way home John said that, "Yes, we need to move out but it will take time." Even though we were both scared out of our wits, apart from psychologically and emotionally neither of us had been harmed. He said let's acknowledge it, treat it like a family member. I thought, *"He's lost the plot now."*

John: I just thought, let's be nice to it. It wants attention. Then let's give it attention. Treat it like a naughty child that has tantrums. I didn't want to dabble in Ouija boards or hold a séance but let's just talk to it. I know, I know, it sounds nuts but what else were we to do?

Sarah: In work that day I cried so much, my manager took me to one side and said she thought that someone had died or that John and I'd had a row or we'd split up. I said I was just stressed and things were tough on us. We finished work and walked home, as we were near the house. It's already dark; it gets dark around five that time of year and it was about 5:30. John said to me, simply smile and be brave. I have to say I was beyond the ability to smile and be positive, but now telling you, in hindsight, it was a good thing for John to say. He suffered so much with anxiety and depression, yet he was determined we could get over this during the time it took for us to get out. We got through the front door and into the living room; I was always frightened that there would be a figure stood there. Imagine the feeling of dread you would have if every time you opened your front door you expected something terrible to be waiting for you. It would make you a wreck, so John flicks on the light and in a big cheery voice said, *"Hello, we're home."*

John: I just started talking to it, talking out loud asking if it had had a nice day, how excited we were to be home and how great it was that we were sharing this amazing house together. I bet people are laughing at that, but what are you going to do? Get Chuck Norris with a crucifix in? No.

Sarah: John was walking around the house just talking like there was someone there, the same way you would if you went over to a friend's house. I was still terrified as you just didn't know what to expect and our poor cat was stuck in there 24/7. If that cat could talk I bet he could tell some stories. John lights some incense sticks, puts on all the lamps and puts the kettle on and looked over at me and said with this big dumb grin of his, *"Green tea?"* I just started laughing and crying and gave him a big hug.

John: You have no idea how anxious we were before bed but we both made a point of saying things like, *"Goodnight, see you in the morning,"* and I said, *"Try and keep it down if you can."*

Sarah: And that night not a peep.

John: Nothing at all happened that night, even the bathroom seemed warmer and less threatening. Either the entity had exhausted itself with its antics the night before or just acknowledging it had miraculously worked.

Sarah: We both went to work a bit more refreshed and brighter the next day, and it stopped for quite a bit.

John: It got to the stage that I was happy to be nice to it. I'd do daft things like ask if it wanted a tea, say things like, *"Right I'm off to the loo, you stay out here."* Just silly stuff but it was working and the house seemed really nice in that it was how a house should be. I was anxious as Sarah had a few weekends away before Christmas for parties and girls' nights out but I felt a bit more relaxed about the house.

Sarah: We had friends coming over one weekend and then I was away for a few weekends. I felt guilty for leaving John behind but he seemed more in control. He was less depressed and was not drinking as much, and the house was behaving. I thought it would be OK. He reassured me that he and Lucky would be fine, and to enjoy myself.

John: One day I was out and about in the garden and under the shed I noticed all these little bones. I thought it was a rat's nest and I hate rats; I'm terrified of them. When I was little, about six or seven, my aunty and her friend took me daffodil picking at this old ruined cottage down the lane near her house, thrilling I know. While they were picking, I went into the old cottage and the floor looked like it was moving. It was full of rats; I fell down the steps and fell face first amongst them. They all scurried around me and over me as they tried to escape. It scared me. I can't abide them even though they did nothing wrong or bit me or anything. If I was a billionaire now I would probably be a superhero called RATMAN. Anyway, I tell Sarah and she says she will call pest control or the council or whoever it was to sort them out.

Sarah: We were leaving the house one Saturday morning to go shopping and we bump into the lady who lives next door. We never saw her or her husband as they both work nights and occasionally we see them leaving or arriving from work. We start chatting and she welcomes us and says if we need anything to just pop in but they mainly sleep all day and work nights. She was nice and polite and friendly. She starts talking to us about how lovely the house is and how deceptively large the garden is.

John: We are talking about the house and garden. I say it's lovely but we have found some little friends and the council is coming to sort them out, and I was referring to the rats.

Sarah: John was talking about the rats in the shed and the woman obviously had misunderstood and she frowned and asked, *"What, the council are taking care of it?"* And John said that they were, that they were coming on Monday. The woman looked dumbfounded and John said, *"Rats, we got rats,"* and she went, *"Oh! I thought you meant the ghosts."*

John: I said, *"What do you mean?"* I was shaking. It was like I had been punched in the stomach. The woman said that at one time our houses had been one house and that our side was haunted by a woman and possibly a child but on their side, in their home, they had a very, very powerful haunting. It was a man who was angry all the time; she believed that all the spirits did cross over into both houses. I couldn't believe it. Part of me was relieved as we were not alone and we were not mad, but knowing that it was real made it more frightening, if that makes sense?

Sarah: She told us that when they first moved in, there was this weird blurry object moving around downstairs that you could not look at directly. The object was about six and a half, maybe even seven feet tall. I was stunned and I told her we had the same but it was small, maybe two or three feet tall. She said that we were lucky and that was probably just the child.

John: Being told a child is haunting your home is one of the most miserable and dismal things I have ever been told, plus their shadow-blur thing was seven feet tall! I don't know what was worse! I felt so sorry for our neighbours.

Sarah: At one stage I started giggling when we were comparing the antics – the cold spots, check. Footsteps, yep, ours does that. That there is a menacing feeling that something is watching you when on the loo or having a shower, check. Thinking you have been burgled in the night, tick that one off. It was almost a relief to be discussing it with someone who understood, who could relate to what we were experiencing.

John: Then she told us that one night her husband had been sat there on his own and he saw what seemed to be the outline of a very tall man very slowly come down the stairs, almost one step at a time, very deliberately. It then entered their living room area, stood there for a few seconds like it was surveying the room, and it just moved and sat in the armchair opposite him, like it was just staring at him. This thing had no discernible features, just a shadowy outline and this was with the light on! The poor guy freaked and ran out of the house, and called his brother and would not go in at all!

It was bad enough with everything that had happened. That I could not handle. I asked her how they coped, how she was so calm about it, and her advice was get a night job or don't be in the house at night. She said on days off they would go and stay with friends and that they were currently looking to rent out the place. It got so bad that she and husband nearly spilt up as the pressure was so intense.

They called it the Angry Man as it would go mad in the night slamming doors and cupboards. If they have ironed some clothes and hung them up then literally a few minutes later they would all be in a pile on the floor. It smashed a picture of her husband's parents, which really upset them. They claimed it had smashed plates and cups in the night. We were fortunate as that hadn't happened to us. I made a joke that perhaps the ghost was Greek and no one laughed.

Sarah: I told her that John has started talking to it, treating it like it was part of the family and that we're housemates in a way. The woman smiled and said if it worked then great, but normally it would go quiet for a while as it was recharging getting ready to do its next thing. She had read books and been online and looked into ghosts and spirits. She said that the night we thought someone had broken in took a lot of energy for the spirit to do and it would need more energy to manifest.

John: I was cross. I believed that we were treating it with respect and that's all it needed. Deep down I hoped all these ghosts would just piss off into hers if she was working nights and party it up, but that was a wrong thing to wish. This poor woman and her husband had been traumatised just like we were and they thought that we were the lucky ones! They had to work their entire lives around it just to stay together. Those poor, poor people, I feel sorry for them.

Sarah: A problem shared is a problem halved, I guess. We chatted for about an hour and we all had to go, and John and I walked into town and I knew he was furious. He needed to believe what we were doing was working and that we had everything under control. We went shopping as our friends were coming over in the evening to stay and John hit the wine aisle. I thought, no, please don't lose it, not now, not when we felt like we were winning. As soon as we got home he started on the wine and he looked sullen. He looked just like the woman who used to own this house, the woman in August with the child; he looked like he had surrendered.

Rob and Emma are the friends in question that stayed that evening with John and Sarah. I was fortunate and grateful that they both gave the time to participate in the investigative interviews. Both currently reside in England, and that night is still clear in their minds even after a decade has passed since the incident. Here is their account of what they believed happened that night.

Emma: I've been friends with Sarah for years, since primary school, and when I went to university I met Rob and we settled down away. We were down for a few weeks in Pembrokeshire for Christmas and Sarah said to stay over one weekend, see the house. She sounded really down. I thought maybe she and John were having relationship issues.

Rob: I met John and Sarah at the odd wedding and get-together and I liked them both. John was easy-going, one of those guys that will make you feel welcome and after a few hours you feel like you've known him forever. That year we decided that we would be staying with Emma's family as we had stayed with mine the year before. I thought it would be nice to have a 'session' with John and Sarah.

Emma: We got to this nice little terraced house, small on the outside, but had an abundance of character. Sarah answered the door and she gave me the biggest hug ever. I thought she was going to break my ribs! As I said I've known her for years and she is a very confident and strong person, but she seemed vulnerable that day. We walked inside this lovely house; it was deceptively large and the outside did not do it justice. I loved the fireplace and the way the house just stretched so far back. John was there in the kitchen and I have to say he was steaming.

Rob: John was hammered! I laughed as he staggered out with a big glass of wine in one hand and half a bottle of wine in the other. Sarah just put a brave face on but you could sense she was furious with him.

Emma: I thought, Christ, John, it's 4pm and you're a mess.

Rob: He was still chatty though. His words slurred but he asked us how we were and if we wanted a drink. I thought when in Rome, and John and I headed into the kitchen and he just handed me a bottle of wine and said to crack on with that.

Emma: Sarah said she would show me around the house. It was really nice, and we went up to the bedroom and she closed the door and started crying. She was sat on the bed and I just hugged her and she shook and sobbed, and I said, "What's wrong?" She said she couldn't live in the house anymore. My first reaction was that she and John had not been getting along; maybe they'd had a big bust-up that day hence John hitting the wine so early. This was not my friend that I had seen grow up to be so strong. This was not the friend who called me a few months previously, so excited and proud, to say John and she were buying a house. She looked thin and pale, a shell of the vibrant person I knew.

Rob: John was fine downstairs; he asked me about work and how Ems and I were getting on. He told some jokes and he just kept drinking.

Emma: Sarah told me that it wasn't John so much but the house; the house was ruining them. Again I thought, "Bills, the pressure of living together." You know, all of the issues you get when you settle down? But Sarah said that there was something wrong with the house and she didn't know what to do and John had given up and no one would believe her and they were scared. I tried to reassure her but we were at cross purposes and then she angrily shouted, *"It's haunted, Em, it's fucking haunted,"* and cried hysterically.

Rob: Emma was upstairs chatting with Sarah and I said, "Could I use the toilet?" John pointed at it and slurred, "In there, but it's haunted," then he laughed his head off. I just thought it was John being John, and he meant that it was haunted as he had been in there earlier and had made a bad smell or something.

Emma: She told me everything that had happened and I will tell you now that it was something I didn't believe in. I told her that everything has a rational explanation but she said, "Not this time." I did not feel anxious or frightened and I told her that if the house was haunted that Rob and I were here now and if anything happened in the night that we would find an explanation for it, and if by some weird chance it was haunted then we would look for a solution. Colour returned to her face and she thanked me over and over. Sarah composed herself and we went back downstairs.

Rob: We had a good night. Sarah cooked us a wonderful meal, such an amazing cook, and John kept the wine flowing and it was fun. We played board games and had some music on, and had a laugh. How John can drink so much is an incredible feat. He was steaming when we got there and by eleven or twelve that night he had polished off another two bottles, maybe three, but he was still chatty and having a laugh. I think I would have been sick.

Emma: It was a good night. Sarah was more relaxed, and she and John seemed happy together. Rob at this time had no idea what had been happening in the house so he thought it was just a usual night. John drank a very serious amount, I was worried, but it's his life. Around midnight or one, it was late, we called it a day and all of us were the worse for wear. Sarah shows us the den where we were to be sleeping on the sofa bed. I knew what happened to her nephew in there and I was not scared at all. In fact I liked the idea that I would be an investigator and I might find an explanation, and Sarah would be happy. I didn't tell Rob at all as it was between Sarah and myself.

Rob: I had no idea what had been happening at the house. We went to bed and I could hear Sarah saying to John that he'd had enough to drink and it was time for bed. John was saying one more and then he would be up, and Sarah was telling him off saying that he was going to spend all night drinking and then be hungover and grumpy the next day. I heard someone storm up the stairs and I presumed that it was Sarah.

Emma: I heard the main bedroom door close, and downstairs I could hear the cupboard or a fridge open and a glass clink. I thought, *"Ah John is on an all-nighter then?"* and I felt sorry for Sarah. Anyway I must have dropped off as I woke to hear John talking quite loudly downstairs and I thought Sarah had got up to try and get him to bed. I sat up and Rob was already awake and he whispered, "He has been talking to someone for ten minutes." I quietly asked was it Sarah and he said he didn't think so, and I then asked was John on the phone.

Rob: I knew nothing about the house at this time, but I could hear John saying things like, *"We live here now."* And, *"We have to try and live together, we're really scared by you."* And I thought he was on the phone. I looked at my watch and it was around 3am.

Emma: I thought he must have been on the phone as I could only hear him talking. He was pleading at one stage, saying that Sarah was his world and he was losing her and that they had nowhere else to go.

Rob: John said something like, *"Please, just leave us,"* and this voice like an old angry woman shouted, *"YOU LEAVE!"* I heard John start to cry and Emma told me to get up and see if he was OK. I didn't fancy it to be honest; it was none of my business.

Emma: As John was talking, this woman's voice, raspy and old, very Welsh, started to shout over him and you could hear John crying. I told Rob to get up and find out what was going on. Who the hell was in the house at 3am? Was it a neighbour or a family member? I clearly heard an old lady shouting at John.

Rob: I banged my head standing up in the spare room but made my way to the door and on to the landing. From there you could hear John crying and talking more clearly. He was saying things between sobs like, *"You evil old Bitch,"* and *"You selfish fuck."* And I heard the voice again interrupt him and say, *"GET OUT!"*

I cleared the stairs in next to no time and John was passed out, asleep on the settee down there. There was no one else down there at all apart from John. I even checked the front door and the back door.

Emma: When Rob made his way down you could hear John shouting at this woman and the woman telling him to get out, but Rob said that John was passed out on the settee. I got up and John was passed out, snoring heavily. It took Rob ages to wake him up and he looked all bleary eyed and drunk and said, "What time is it?"

Rob: I don't know if it was a prank by John, but the old woman sounded like she was a few feet from the bottom of the stairs and John was over by the storage unit. I was shocked to see him passed out. We went back to bed and left him there.

Emma: In the morning I told Sarah, who hadn't heard a thing. I asked her straight was all this ghost shit a prank, and if it was that I didn't find it funny especially at three in the morning. She in all fairness looked genuinely confused and she started crying, saying that she didn't know what had happened and had no idea what John had been up to. I don't know if there was someone in there with John, or if it had been a recording but it was a strange night.

John and Sarah swore it was nothing to do with them and at breakfast we were all quiet. I told Sarah that we would stay at my mum's that night instead of going out for dinner and staying again. Sarah was aghast and pleaded that we stay. John said he had no idea what had happened, and whatever it was, that he was sorry and that he would keep sober that night. We left and it wasn't until about a year later that Sarah and I started talking properly again. She is convinced that something happened in that house but it's not for me to say what is haunted or not haunted.

I've had no experiences or seen anything that would make me believe any differently. Psychological issues, tiredness, booze, smoking pot, all these things can make people believe in things that aren't there. I never went back to the house when Sarah lived there but I would walk back in there tomorrow and not bat an eyelid.

Rob: It was only afterwards that Emma told me about what had been happening there. She wouldn't have any of it; but I heard two distinct people downstairs and John's voice was anguished and the way the old woman shouted at him does chill me. I liked John and I miss him, but hey that's life.

John: I have no idea what happened that night. Last thing I remember was getting another bottle from the kitchen after everyone had gone to bed. I drank that and passed out. I don't remember having a conversation or row with an old woman and if that is what Rob and Ems heard then that's what they heard, but I swear to you now and to anyone out there that reads this and makes sense of it all, that I did not hoax it or have a recording or get someone to come into our house at 3am to piss about. We had enough on our plate without all that added to it.

I got drunk and I passed out, and then everyone shouted at me and blamed me.

Sarah: I didn't hear anything. When Ems and Rob left I knew I'd had enough, enough of the house, of working to keep it all together and most of all I had enough of John. I hated him, I hated him so much. If he hadn't got drunk that day and had just come to bed then maybe all that wouldn't have happened. Maybe, if he hadn't been so weak and selfish and crawled into his bottle like a coward because our neighbour told him something that he didn't like or agree with, then that night would not have happened. Emma and I would not have fallen out for a year and maybe things could have got better. I made a conscious effort that day to change my life.

John: Sarah was mad about that day and the drinking, not just that night but in general. I saw coldness in her eyes. She had cut me loose. I was just some pathetic drunk, not man enough to support her and help her deal with this. I'm not looking for the sympathetic vote but anyone out there that has become dependent on alcohol when they are stressed or anxious will understand how I felt. I felt so helpless. It was not as if I could just click my fingers and go back in time. If I could do things differently then, yes, I would but at the time the wine and the drink was my coping mechanism. I don't drink at all now; too little too late I guess. Until you have lived in that situation with everything as berserk as it was then no one can tell me how to cope or how to behave.

I honestly hope that if someone out there reads this and is experiencing the same as we did then, at least use this as a cautionary tale. Just get out, just leave. Stay with friends, family or even sleep in a car, but don't stay and be a victim. You can't beat it, you cannot win. It chooses when it's done, and we can't understand its agenda or its endgame. The sad thing was that wasn't the end. There was more in store for us.

Sarah: I didn't speak to him much at all that week. It was awful. I saw him in work and I saw him at home. He tried to talk to me on the Sunday and Monday and I just blanked him. He slept in the den with the light on. I was furious with him and I was out that weekend with friends and I wouldn't be back until Sunday night, and I didn't care what happened to him and the house.

John: She really turned the screw on me, and I tried to talk things through. She was having none of it. You know what? Nothing happened in the house that week, nothing at all. It was like it was enjoying the tension between us; it was happy to see us fall apart.

Sarah: On the Friday, I left straight from work with my friend. I didn't text John or even call him that weekend.

John: When she went off that Friday, my first plan was to get hammered. Hit the wine aisle… fuck it! What's the point? But I thought no, I would sober up and when Sarah came back Sunday night the house would be clean and tidy and I would be sober and in control. The house would be the way it was when I was acknowledging the spirit, entity, whatever it was. I was scared of being on my own, especially after our friends had been telling us I had been arguing with some old woman in the middle of the night. Plus, it hadn't been that long since we thought we had been burgled. My plan was just to keep it together till Sarah came home, plus I had Lucky the cat to keep me company too. She needed a break and I hoped she would come home, regretful and sorry that we had fallen apart and we'd try even harder this time. This time, I would sober up. Friday night nothing happened apart from the feeling in the bathroom again and I just said, *"Night night now, sleep well,"* and I went to bed and kept the light and Radio 4 on.

I woke up and dawn was breaking and I was happy. I had survived the night. I had breakfast and nipped into Haverfordwest, got a few bits and bobs and thought I would cook a dinner for Sarah and me for Sunday night. I texted her but had no reply. I felt so sad inside but I just hoped she was OK, and we'd talk about it when she came home. That night I watched some TV and then I was sat at the dining table reading a book and drinking green tea. Yeah, look at me all civilised and sober! I'm reading with some music quietly in the background, it was *Melody A.M.* by Royksopp, a nice chilled album. I had texted Sarah again, but nothing. It's about 10pm and I hear footsteps in the den and I was thinking, *"No, no, not now,"* and it was the same as before, like ladies' heels. It started at the end where the boiler door was and made its way to the other side. Then back, and slowly and clearly it slammed what could only be the boiler door three times. Bam… Bam… Bam.

I sat there staring at the ceiling with my hairs on end. Nothing happened for ages. Then slowly the footsteps started back across the den, very, very slowly. They got to where the den door was and I heard the latch go and the door swing open. For whatever reason, rather than run into the street or something I rushed to the bottom of the stairs and at the top of the landing was Lucky, he had made himself all big, hair standing up, hissing at something. I managed to call, *"Lucky."* He bolted down the stairs and hid behind the settee. I ran too and stood by the living room door that led to the hall, front door and the safety of the street.

My heart was pounding in my head. I went outside on the street for a bit and paced about. A few people passed on the way into or out of town. I got myself together, went back in and turned the TV on. It was as loud as I could get it. I made sure all the downstairs lights were on and sat bolt upright on the settee. Over the din of the TV I could hear what sounded like the upstairs being turned upside down. I heard multiple footsteps running around in the den, the latch and the doors opening and closing. I don't think I have ever felt so alone and miserable in my life. It only lasted maybe thirty seconds, maybe a bit more. I cried so much that night. I wanted Sarah home.

Sarah: I don't know exactly what happened to John that

night, but when I came home Sunday he tried to act casual. He tried to hug me and be nice, but I'd had a great weekend. I felt free and fresh and young and excited again. I came back to the *ball and chain* that was John and the house. He made me feel sick. I know he tried and he'd made dinner and claimed not to have drunk all weekend but my eyes had been opened. New things were starting to come into my life, and it was too late for John and me. He briefly spoke about that night, much later on, and it sounded awful but part of me still blames him anyway.

John: I know Sarah blames me for so much, but I don't know how I got ghosts into the house or how drinking wine conjures up poltergeist activity. If I could do that then I would be a millionaire or working for the CIA. It was already there and she wanted the house so badly. Her friend should have bloody well told her it was haunted. Ask yourself, would you not buy a house because someone said it's haunted? Of course not, it's ludicrous and I'm sad that it all went wrong for us, but I do blame the house. People can say, *"Yeah, but you were pissed all the time."* I, we were happy before in the flat, I'm sure we were. You can't unravel what's already been done but we were happy back then before that awful, miserable house.

Sarah: It was probably the worst Christmas you could imagine. We put no decorations up and John was, pardon the pun, like a ghost. I guess he tried to put a brave face on it, but we were essentially over. Every opportunity I could, I spent away. Was I selfish? Perhaps, but John had just as much chance to stay away. One night, I was in bed and he was lying on the sofa in a sleeping bag, sobbing, and I thought, *"Just grow up, stop being such a child."*

John: I have wonderful and remarkable friends, but back then they had young families. They were always kind and offering to let me stay over, but it's their time. They don't need some sad, lonely man ruining their Christmas and I don't have much of a family. I just hoped Sarah and I could work it through. I wasn't stupid; I knew she was staying with other men. I just hoped I would wake up and it had all been a nightmare and we would be back in the flat, it would be summer again and we would never, ever leave.

Sarah: John was acting strange. I was going to stay with my parents for Christmas Day and on Christmas Eve John gives me a load of presents like everything was OK. Then out of the blue, he put out a mince pie and a glass of sherry. Not for Father Christmas, no, that would have been perfectly acceptable. No, he put it out for the ghost. He even wrote it a card.

John: I just thought maybe the house would have appreciated it. People are probably laughing; it's actually one of the few things from that time that I laugh about to this day. I was hoping to find some ectoplasm in my stocking. I didn't see much of Sarah over Christmas and I just spent it on my own. I didn't drink, I swear. I just texted her each day and hoped she would let me back in, back into her thoughts. I just hoped she would let me back into her heart.

I was empty and heartbroken, that hollow hurt in your stomach just below your chest. It's so sad. It was the first time I had been hurt by someone; it was terrible. You think, you wish you could go to sleep and wake up and be someone else, someone better or at least not wake up at all. Sadly some people out there will know how that feels. There was not a peep from the house, nothing. It was like it was just watching, and observing me as I became more and more entrenched in my depression.

Sarah: I came back the day after New Year's Eve. I decided John had to leave and I would keep the house on till we could rent it out. I came back early and John was not in the house. He'd left a note saying he was going to spend a night with his friends in Neyland. I was happy with that, they were good to him. It gave me more time working out how I was going to talk to him about everything. I was planning to effectively throw him out of his own home. A friend of mine had explained to me my entitlement, and basically, John didn't really have a leg to stand on. He was broke so there was no way he could fight me legally. I must sound like a right cow, but people have no idea how tough it was on me back then.

I'd fed the cat and was on the mobile chatting to this guy I had met over Christmas, and I lit a candle on the mantelpiece. The mantelpiece was massive and an old-fashioned brick style; it had probably been there from when the house was built. In the centre was this antique candlestick John had got from this old place on the High Street. I went into the kitchen and poured myself a glass of wine; I was surprised that John had left any. I turned back and the living room was full of smoke. I dashed in and a wastepaper basket we used to keep incense sticks in was on fire and right in the middle was the candle. I ran into the kitchen and soaked a dishcloth and put the fire out. I opened the windows and then the smoke alarm went off.

I was shaking. Somehow the candle had fallen out of the candle stick, rolled three maybe four feet along the top of the mantelpiece, leaping a foot or two and landing in the wastepaper basket. I knew deep down what it was. What if I had gone upstairs or to the bathroom? I could have been killed.

John: I didn't know at the time what had happened until a day later. It terrifies me now. Bangs, footsteps and cold spots and the like are one thing. This sounded too strange to just be an accident. Maybe it was pissed off with Sarah or maybe it was mad that I didn't spend the night there. The day after my friends dropped me off in Haverfordwest, I walked past this shop where I bought incense sticks, and popped in. They were doing fortunes or tarot that day. I'm having a browse and this woman says, *"You have a very dark shadow following you."* I thought, how charming.

I asked her what she meant by that. She explained to me that she was a psychic medium. Immediately I thought, not now, not interested, not after what had happened with the blessing and what a spectacular disaster that had been. I gave the woman the time of day though, just because I needed all the help I could get back then. Suddenly, she went all gypsy fortune-teller on me and said that I had spoken to the woman whose spirit resided in the house, that it was not her but one of the child spirits that had set fire to the house but it had been an accident. I thought what was she was on about? There had been no fire.

It's obvious now, but I hadn't been home yet and I hadn't spoken to Sarah. I told her about the night when my friends had heard me have a conversation with what sounded like an old lady. The woman didn't seem to be surprised; she didn't look at me like I had two heads. She then said it was a woman and two children, and that a very hateful man would sometimes enter the house. He was the scary one, the one who made all the noise. She had me engrossed and I bought into what she was saying. I asked her what could I do and she said to buy this crystal glass thing and she said to wash it and place it on the mantelpiece. I didn't tell her we already had one, but being psychic she no doubt knew anyway, and that the spirits would use it to muster enough energy to leave. What did I have to lose? Well, forty quid but it had to be worth it. If it got rid of the spirits or should I say help the spirits leave for a higher spiritual plane then maybe I could get Sarah back. I ran home that day, hopeful.

Sarah: I decided not to stay that night after the candle, fed the animals and stayed at a friend's. He picked me up and as he drove off he said that he thought he saw a little girl wave from the window. I told him he must have been imagining things. The next day I get home and a few minutes after I get in, John barges in all excited, babbling that everything was going to be OK. He tried to hug me but I told him to back off. He told me about this woman and what she'd said, and he showed me this big green crystal.

John: I ran into the kitchen and washed it as the woman had told me to do, and placed it on the mantelpiece. I knew, I just knew that this would work; I just needed Sarah to give me some time. I thought it had to be worth something to her. I needed her to have some fight, just a little, enough to give this and us a chance. If not then let's call it a day, but in life you got to fight for what's worth living for, for what makes you happy, the things that make you glad to be alive.

Sarah: John practically got on his hands and knees and begged me to just give him a week, to give us a week and he swore that everything that was happening in the house would stop. I told him he had a week to find somewhere else to live as we were finished and I'd met someone else.

John: I remember her telling me. You have this feeling, all the way from the base of your spine to the pit of your stomach. It felt like I had been gutted, probably where the expression comes from. It's crippling, it's everything in one big glorious ball of shit. It was anger, denial, jealousy, bitterness and a childlike feeling of just wanting to hide and cry. It had taken just three months in the house for it to end. I was furious. I demanded to know who it was, promised I would ruin whoever it was. It was just words as it was too late. It was over.

Sarah: I explained to John what would be happening, that he would leave and I would stay a short time, told him what he had to do and he put up no fight. A week later he was back at his dad's and then he signed the house over to me and gave me his key. He took his things; he didn't have much to be honest.

John: That last week was heartbreaking but I was right, that woman in the shop was right; the house was quiet, not a cold spot, or a feeling of menace or a footstep in the night. The crystal works. I can't explain to you how, but it works. I read afterwards that you can surround or fill an object with positive energy and create a powerful talisman to protect you. You could do it with a button if you believed in it enough.

Sarah: The night John left I was sad, but it was no good to either of us to live together. The house had been peaceful that week, serene almost. I felt that we could move on with our lives, that we'd both be OK and in time maybe we could be friends. Whatever John had been on about regarding the ghosts moving on was right. Then I was in store for the worst night of my life. I went to bed at around ten. The house was quiet, warm and cosy. I read for a bit, texted a bit and I dropped off. I woke up and the bedroom door was wide open. I had fallen asleep with the light on and I could have sworn I'd closed the door. Then I felt the most chilling and intense coldness I have ever experienced. I could see my breath in front of my face. Then I felt the duvet slowly start to slip away from me. I held it tight and pulled it up to my chin and then something grabbed my foot and pulled... I... I screamed and screamed. I screamed for John.

John: It all started up again the night I left. It was probably because I took that crystal with me. It cost me forty quid. I'm sure her new bloke could get her a new one. He seemed to be giving her plenty of other things if you know what I mean.

Sarah: It was awful. Everything was intensified. This was no nightmare or hallucination. It grabbed me. I hardly spent a night there since. I moved out and luckily not too long afterwards I managed to rent the place out but people don't stay long. Thankfully they've been contractors from the refineries or students from the college. Now and again when someone asks to terminate their tenancy after only a few months, deep down I know why, but I never ask and I never mention it when new people come to view the property. I know how that woman must have felt when John and I came to view the property that day. She must have been so relieved to leave. There was not a chance in hell that she was going to mention it and neither am I. Some close friends have said that I am obliged, that I should tell people, but really? Would anyone out there believe it if they were told a house was so haunted that it might destroy their lives? No, you would look insane.

I need the money as the mortgage won't pay itself. You asked me earlier about the people that live there now and you asked me was it my responsibility to protect them, to tell them. For all I know the house might have stopped or they might be happy there. It's not for me to say and even if they ask then I will say no, that I don't know what they are on about. You can't blame me for that. I don't speak much to John. I dropped him a message when you got in touch, when I saw your letter, and I have a family now and am happily married. What happened before is just a small part of my life. You move on and in time you start to forget. It's only natural to move on. I can't give anyone an explanation of what was happening at that house. Some people have easy answers but they aren't there. Some will say that it's made-up; made-up for what? So I can look like a nutter? Made-up so that I can't live in my house? It was very real to me and it totally fucked John up. All we have to do is look back and be relieved that it's over. It's done; apart from a few visits a year I have very little to do with the house.

John: Ten years is a long time. I try not to pass the house if I can help it. I know it's haunted, it is, really. OK, you can say: define a haunting. You see movies now like *Paranormal Activity*, with demons, movies about aliens. But a haunting to me is when something beyond our understanding inhabits a home, and the people in it can't comprehend what is happening. There is no solution, no help, and no magic wand to make it leave. Science and religion can't make it stop; it's a powerful force that no one can persuade to leave. It holds all the cards. I can't think of a rational explanation for such an intense and traumatic experience. It was prolonged and it was at times truly terrifying. It drove Sarah and I apart.

She and I are the ghosts now. Do you know, I saw her the other day by chance in the street, and we said a quiet hello and kept walking; we are strangers. There is no bond there, no connection. It used to make me sad thinking of how happy we were and how complete my life felt. Now it's nothing more than a dark memory. I don't regret losing the house, not in the slightest. I am blessed to have no ties to that place. I was just another plaything or victim to the entity, depending on how you look at it. When I left and went back to my dad's, I worried that it would follow me but I have moved plenty in the last ten years and I make sure that I always have that piece of green crystal with me. I never want that thing back in my life.

I will never step foot in that house again as long as I live, and I genuinely hope and pray that whoever is living there now has a much easier time than us. You've got to ask yourself, all these couples having a terrible time of it, arguing all the time. Maybe, just maybe it's because of entities, spirits, whatever you want to call them. There, driving them apart for whatever reason these things do it for. We can't fathom their motives. I took hundreds of photos while I was there and nothing showed up. We had the house blessed and it made it worse. People came to our home and were badly affected. There is no safety in numbers. Science can't explain it. You're dealing with something on an entirely different level. If this is happening to you then get out, get out now. You can't fight it, you won't win and you'll end up losing everything that matters to you. If you hear our story, don't be harsh on us and call us frauds or weirdos; and if it does happen to you or it's happening then like I say, just get out, get out before it's too late and you lose everything.

Summary of Possible Explanations

It is only expected that we try and make sense of the testimonials presented in this tome. The following explanations are not intended to insult sceptic or believer but are bestowed to give you possible explanations on the causes. These will include rational, psychological and the transcendental. We touch upon Toxic Mould to Demonology, from Psychedelics to Time Rifts and ideas to give you plenty of food for thought to reread and re-ponder the events at the house.

Some of these theories can explain all the paranormal symptoms experienced, while some only parts. They may contradict each other and will certainly open up new possibilities for the events. I am not endorsing any of these ideas as categorically correct; rather than merely introducing them to you. Some you will be familiar with and others you may appreciate as a new hypothesis.

Please note that each hypothesis will have a great number of books written about the research behind them, therefore, this is just a summary to give you a brief understanding. Also, these are not all the possible explanations behind the events. These are a few to digest and explore. These are not necessarily my direct theories either but ones I have researched. I have included the sources for the information should you wish to continue investigating.

As mentioned in this volume I humbly concede that I am a self-educated man with learning difficulties so I have attempted to translate the theories as simply as possible. This is not intended to patronise you, the reader, but to simply help myself make sense of the information researched.

Until a day comes where the house can be fully investigated we only have the personal testimonials of the people who have lived there to process. Please feel free to contact me if you have any ideas or theories on the strange occurrences at that house in

Haverfordwest, or if you have experienced something similar that you do have an explanation for.

Let us start with the mundane and work our way towards the mind-bending.

Toxic Mould Theory

Ghosts tend to be sighted in old buildings, which are often more likely to have damp and mould problems. No one is exactly sure of the psychoactive effects of indoor moulds on the brain, but spores have been linked with mood swings, hyperactivity, and irrational anger, as well as cognitive impairment. Recent reports indicate that exposure to toxic mould spores may cause brain inflammation and memory loss. A team of researchers is exploring whether the mould may cause people to think they have seen ghosts, by comparing conditions in 'haunted' and non-haunted old buildings. Here, presented, is an article on the research currently being conducted into this theory.

Researchers claim that older buildings where hauntings are usually reported often have poor air quality from pollutants like toxic mould, which can affect our brains. Exposure to the mould can cause mood swings, irrational anger and cognitive impairment. "Experiences reported in many hauntings are similar to mental or neurological symptoms reported by individuals exposed to toxic moulds," said Professor Shane Rogers of Clarkson University in Potsdam, New York. "Psychoactive effects of some fungi are well-known, whereas the effects of others such as indoor moulds are less researched."

Other reports include depression and loss of memory function. More recent work is emerging that supports brain inflammation and memory loss in mice exposed to Stachybotrys charatarum, a common indoor air mould, as well as increased anxiety and fear.

Professor Rogers is currently leading a team of researchers measuring air quality in several reportedly haunted places around New York State. The group will compare samples taken from several buildings where ghost sightings have been reported with samples taken from properties with no paranormal activity, to see if there is a difference in the types of fungi.

Professor Rogers said: "I have long been a fan of ghost stories and shows related to an investigation of haunted places and have to admit to some strange occurrences in my own past. Many of the places under investigation and from my own experiences may be prime environments for mould and other indoor air quality issues. We would like to see if we can parse out some commonality between the mould microbiome in places that are haunted relative to those that are not."

The team has only just begun their investigations but has been to a handful of 'haunted' buildings to collect samples, as well as properties with mould, but no connection to ghosts.

"In one historic house turned into an office building there have been reports of noises, moving ceiling tiles, moving items on shelves and desks, apparitions, and a general feeling of unease among building occupants," he said.

There have been long-standing stories of some of the original family members still occupying the place.

"In another location, the Remington Art Museum in Ogdensburg, New York, there is a long history of ghost stories involving the former occupants and others. A week prior to our visit, they had a visit from a psychic who took a reading in several rooms in the museum that we then used to target our air quality studies. She reported a few 'folks' came to speak with her, children running in and out of some of the rooms in the house and a woman that claimed she was 'not won in a poker game', which was related to a long-time story related to the Remington family. So far, we haven't been spooked out of a location, but time will tell."

Source: Daily Mail 2nd *April 2015*

Anne had seen mildew or mould on the ceiling of the living room that Rose claimed was due to the presence of the entity. Could it be possible that spores from the mould were being breathed in changing perceptions and amplifying the feeling of an unseen force?

I personally had not seen much evidence of mould. However, I was not looking for it and it was not a theory I was aware of at the time of the events, but one that requires further investigation.

Terrestrial Trunked Radio

I always found this theory to be one that needed much investigation. In the early 2000s a new and controversial communications system was placed in Haverfordwest for use by the emergency services. Immediately there were concerns from locals with protests and petitions, and a public awareness campaign was created in an attempt to stop this device from being used. Initial complaints were ignored and the mast was tested. The test coincided with the events of *A most haunted house*, which would not explain the events a decade earlier unless it had been used in secret without the public's knowledge. I myself received a pamphlet discouraging the use of the mast as the technology was allegedly based on Cold War weaponry designed to invoke depression, anxiety and to demoralise enemy troops.

What is TETRA? Terrestrial Trunked Radio (TETRA, formerly known as Trans-European Trunked Radio), a European standard for a trunked radio system, is a professional mobile radio and two-way transceiver specification. TETRA was specifically designed for use by government agencies, emergency services (police forces, fire departments, ambulance) for public safety networks, rail transport staff for train radios, transport services and the military.

There is an interesting and sobering article in the *Ecologist* about TETRA, which at the time was a proposed new system to be used by the police as a communication device to replace walkie-talkies. Here's the first paragraph:

> Costing £2.9 billion, the UK's new police communication system Tetra has been described by one independent scientist as likely to cause "more civilian deaths than all the world's terrorist organisations put together". If you live near a Tetra mast, then this story affects you directly. And considering that there will eventually be at least 3,200 such masts erected in the UK, there will be one near you. Children from Littlehampton in Sussex had to be sent home from school with nosebleeds when the mast was turned on.

Following on is an article published on *TETRAWATCH*, a website that was created to give understanding to the technology and also as a platform to warn of the potential dangers of using such a device:

Wherever, and always, there is something that affects the well-being of people, opportunity is taken for military application. Can you build either some advantage over potential enemies or some better defence understanding in case they get there first? Military 'necessity' and money, backed by governments the world over, has ensured that everything harmful has been explored for weapon potential.

This includes the electromagnetic spectrum, and electromagnetic fields of all kinds, which is why we have the fully documented story of the [US] Embassy in Moscow during the Cold War, and the use of low level pulsed EMF against a civilian population. In addition, we have the known effects, not of weaponry, but of communications and radar systems. A huge amount of knowledge exists in the military on the issues that concern us with TETRA, around the biological effects of microwave radiation.

For many years, unsuspecting populations, both of military

personnel, their families at military bases, and the general population, caught in radar and communications crossfire, have suffered very similar experiences, and worse, to those we describe for TETRA. Include in that the connection between microwave exposure to TETRA-like battlefield communications and Gulf War Syndrome.

For some time very similar concerns have been expressed about military radar sites such as Fylingdales, North Yorkshire. Here we have a clear example of why radiation levels have to stay as high as ICNIRP (or beyond). Can you imagine finding that military sites overexpose populations? To whom do you complain? And would you get a straight answer from Ofcom on actual levels? Supposing it was accepted that research shows biological effects of the ELF frequencies used? Would any civilian campaign get this US-controlled military setup to turn its levels down or change its bio-harmful frequencies? It is almost as if it is not in the interests of 'global security' – as defined by the US – to even acknowledge the dangers to people.

Sources: the Ecologist, TETRAWATCH

The most worrying element of this is the connection to Gulf War Syndrome (GWS), and Gulf War veterans who suffered medically unexplained illnesses. A prominent condition affecting Gulf War veterans is a cluster of medically unexplained chronic symptoms that can include fatigue, headaches, joint pain, indigestion, insomnia, dizziness, respiratory disorders, and memory problems. Could TETRA explain the events in Haverfordwest?

Though little information is available on the exact nature the technology has on the civilian population, I cannot rule out that it may be a very real cause of perceived paranormal incidents. Could it be possible that our brains are unintentionally manipulated by unseen frequencies or waves that cause us to become depressed, irrational and paranoid? Maybe even parts of the brain were stimulated to perceive strange anomalies, smells, sounds and visions? GWS cases have shown that some veterans become unaware of their habits and forget actions carried out in the day. Could it be possible that Sarah, Dai, Anne and I were subconsciously creating the haunting and then genuinely forgetting we had carried out these actions? Were we haunting ourselves? Were we literally responsible, with no knowledge of what we were doing?

How could this TETRA technology be concentrated in one location? This does dissolve the credibility of the theory. However, in recent years I have received reports of similar or general paranormal activity from over a dozen homes in Haverfordwest, and like the house, all of them resided within one mile of where the TETRA mast had been tested.

Localised phenomena

Following on from the TETRA theory is that paranormal activity may be induced by further external as well as internal elements. Melissa Pelletier has conducted much research into these which are presented here for your consideration.

Magnetic fields

In some haunted locations, researchers have measured magnetic fields that are stronger than normal or which exhibit unusual fluctuations. These may be localised phenomena that stem from electronic equipment or geological formations, or they may be part of the Earth's magnetic field. Some paranormal investigators think the presence of strange magnetic fields as proof of a supernatural presence; the ghosts create the field. Others suggest that these fields can interact with the human brain, causing hallucinations, dizziness or other neurological symptoms.

Infrasound

Several experiments have demonstrated that low-frequency

sound waves, known as infrasound, can cause phenomena that people typically associate with ghosts. This includes feelings of nervousness and discomfort as well as a sense of a presence in the room. The sound waves may also vibrate the human eye, causing people to see things that are not there.

Somatosensory

In an attempt to understand why some people have ongoing paranormal experiences, scientists in Switzerland developed an illusion to make healthy people feel a ghostly presence. The results of the simulation were astonishing, revealing that the experience is due to mismatched sensory and motor information that confuses the brain.

The team from the École Polytechnique Fédérale de Lausanne designed a set-up involving two robots – one that sits in front of the participant, and one that sits behind them. Each participant was asked to place their hand on a device and then move their hand around.

Their hand movements were transmitted to the robot sitting behind them, which prompted it to put its hand on the participant's back, mimicking their movements in real-time. This made the participant feel like they were touching their own back, but because the robot was so in-sync with their movements, their brain was able to adapt to the feeling.

Next, the team added a short delay between the participant's hand movements and the robot's touch – and this is where things got interesting. After three minutes of delayed touching, several participants felt that there was someone behind them, and others counted up to four 'ghosts' in the room. Even though the robot was standing behind them, the volunteers were aware of its presence, and still reported the distinct feeling.

"For some, the feeling was even so strong that they asked to stop the experiment," said Giulio Rognini, robotic scientist and one of the team, in a press release. The results suggest that when the robot's touch was out-of-sync with the participant's hand movements, the brain couldn't identify the signals as belonging to the participant's body, but rather as someone else.

The signals of the sensations of touch are a part of the somatosensory system. Processing primarily occurs in the primary somatosensory area in the parietal lobe of the cerebral cortex: information is sent from the receptors via sensory nerves, through tracts in the spinal cord and finally into the brain.

Scientists are taking these findings to help those who experience hallucinations and schizophrenia, but it doesn't exactly explain people's experiences when they have a brain without any disorders. Where does that leave people who have a paranormal experience, but yet can't explain it with science?

Source: Melissa Pelletier nuskool.com

Psychological issues

In *Ghost sex: The Violation* AS Hawking and I presented a number of psychological issues that may be the cause of paranormal perception specifically dealing with concepts of sexual and physical abuse from unseen entities. Here is an excerpt from those notes that relate more to general paranormal events rather than those directly attached to the Pembroke Dock case. For more on psychological issues that may be responsible for the manifestation of a perceived sexual attack see *Ghost sex: The Violation* by GL Davies.

A broad hypothesis would be that they experienced a hallucination. Visual hallucinations involve seeing things that aren't there. The hallucinations may be of objects, visual patterns, people, and/or lights. For example, you might see a person who is not in the room or flashing lights that no one else can see. Hallucinations are sensations that appear real but are created by your mind.

They can affect all five of your senses. You might hear a voice that no one else in the room can hear or see an image that is not real. These symptoms may be caused by mental illness, the side effects of medications, or physical illnesses like epilepsy or alcoholism. Treatment may include taking medication to cure a physical or mental illness or adopting healthier behaviours like drinking less alcohol and getting more sleep.

Hallucinations are false or distorted sensory experiences that seem real and may be seen, heard, felt, and even smelled or tasted, yet are generated only by the mind. A hallucination occurs when a misfire occurs within the mechanism of the brain that helps to distinguish conscious perceptions from internal, memory-based perceptions.

I have known of a case where a woman claimed to hear people in her home and this was always at the time of her period. She was diagnosed with PMMD, the most severe form of premenstrual syndrome, which was affecting her hormonal and brain wave activity and was creating very real hallucinations. A course of medication soon eradicated the symptoms, and the voices ceased to exist.

Sleep states and altered states of consciousness can lead people to believe that they have experienced something supernatural. For example, sceptics have used sleep paralysis or a hypnogogic trance to explain encounters in which people see spirits while in bed and are unable to move or escape. Most people experience a hypnogogic trance once or twice in their lives, although it is far more common in people with epilepsy or certain sleep disorders.

In regards to the sense of people in the house or even shadowy figures being seen in the home, there is research to explain what may be happening. When Swiss scientists electrically stimulated an epileptic patient's brain, the patient reported a shadow person sitting behind her copying her every move. When she sat up, it also sat up. When she bent forward and grabbed her knees, it reached around her body and held her. The doctors then told her to read a card, but the shadow person tried to take it out of her hand. The scientists had stimulated the left temporoparietal junction, the part of the brain that defines the idea of self. By interfering with the area that helps us tell the difference between ourselves and others, the doctors confused the brain's ability to understand its own body, thus leading to the creation of a copycat shadow person. Researchers are hoping this is the key to understanding why so many people, both schizophrenic and healthy, encounter shadow beings and other creatures like aliens.

The idea that experiences of paranormal activity are linked to mental illness is not a new idea. People who see things that others don't see or hear things that others don't hear are, more often than not, going to be seen as something other than normal. While it's true that mental illness can indeed lead someone to believe they're having an experience of the paranormal, this doesn't necessarily mean that everyone who believes they've experienced the paranormal is indeed mentally ill.

One of the most important links between paranormal activity and mental illness comes right from the diagnostic criteria for some mental illnesses. For example, hearing voices is one of the symptoms of schizophrenia, as well as many other mental illnesses. Thus, when someone hears a voice, they immediately qualify for one of the criteria for those particular diagnoses.

However, this doesn't necessarily mean that the person is mentally ill, either. There is more than just a single criterion for mental illnesses. The fact that a person hears a voice (or believes they hear a voice) doesn't automatically guarantee an illness. All it means is that they heard a voice. There are many things that can cause this type of experience.

It's tempting to assume, therefore, that anyone who hears a voice must either be mentally ill or have had a paranormal experience. This isn't the case either. It is entirely possible (and, in the eyes of many, probable) that an otherwise sane individual may experience a momentary sensory hallucination brought on by anything from a bad egg sandwich to an ear infection. That person may come to believe they've had a paranormal experience, and it may lead others to believe the person is mentally ill. In all reality, the person may just have had indigestion.

This, of course, doesn't mean that there are no paranormal experiences. It also doesn't mean that there are. It also doesn't mean that every mentally ill person, whose mental illness includes hallucinations or hearing voices as one of the diagnostic criteria, will experience those particular symptoms.

In the end, the whole question of a link between paranormal experiences and mental illness is only peripherally related. In fact, it's probably best to create a divide between the idea of paranormal experiences and mental illnesses. The link that exists is tenuous, and in many cases, completely irrelevant. The real question of how the individual interprets a given event is what will help determine whether the event was paranormal, psychological, or even neither.

Source: AS Hawking, Ghost sex: The Violation, *theparanormalchronicles.com*

Psychedelics and other drugs

Dai alluded to the notion he suspected he had been drugged. How one would be open to such prolonged exposure to any mind-altering substance is open to conjecture but is a theory that needs further exploration. How would the drug be administered? Without full examination of the house to test the water and the air we can never know. However, study of the effect of drugs and their connection with the paranormal has been conducted.

Psychedelics and paranormal experience have been the study of such a theory by David Luke. David Luke is a parapsychology researcher at the Centre for the Study of Anomalous Psychological Processes, at the University of Northampton in the UK, where he researches paranormal beliefs and experiences, particularly in the context of altered states, such as via dreams and drugs. He and collaborator Marios Kittenis recently published "A preliminary survey of paranormal experiences with psychoactive drugs" in the *Journal of Parapsychology*, which reports on the responses from a 2005 survey of psychedelic drug users.

Here is an excerpt from an interview he conducted regarding his findings:

It would be hard to deny that there are specific neurotransmitter pathways being activated by different drugs, but it would take further research to answer your question directly. This is because it is not yet known whether it is the specific neurochemical action of the drug that causes these experiences directly or whether it is due to the states that they engender. These states may come about through a great variety of means, other than drugs, though it is conceivable that all altered states involve particular neurochemical changes. Nevertheless, these figures represent the percentage of people in the sample ever having these experiences on these drugs at any time in their life. The actual frequency with which they occur is generally quite low, usually just occasionally, although a few experiences seem to occur quite often with specific substances – such as the experience of telepathy with cannabis and plant-entity encounters with psilocybin-containing mushrooms – there might be stronger psychological or even transpersonal explanations for such experiences. You might expect these experiences to be more reliably repeatable if the specific neurochemistry were the only cause. Clearly set, setting, expectation, motivation, and maybe even some fundamentally esoteric properties of our ontology are at work – because these experiences might actually be 'real' in some sense.

One way in which we might begin to distinguish between neurochemical and psychological-state causes of such experiences would be to conduct ESP experiments with people under the influence of a particular drug and compare their performance and experience to people who were reliving the experience under post-hypnotic suggestion. Fortunately, this technique now appears more viable. Arthur Hastings of the Institute of Transpersonal Psychology in California recently published a paper in the *Journal of Psychoactive Drugs* (2006, 38, 273–283) indicating success at re-inducing full MDMA experiences through post-hypnotic suggestion. ESP experiments could be applied to such a technique and begin to answer your question further.

For this study, we defined relaxants as drugs – such as kava and GHB, or GBL – not falling into any of the other categories. Yes, it did surprise us to see that such a group of drugs was the only one to give us any correlation between ESP experience frequency and the reported frequency of consumption, but this relationship was very small and probably artefactual, as there were so few people in our sample reporting use of these substances, and neither was there anyone reporting any specific experiences with these substances. It seems the same artefact may apply for all the correlations between the frequency of relaxant-consumption and paranormal experience, perhaps with the exception of entity-encounter experience. It might seem surprising that this last experience is concomitant with the use of these drugs, but outside of this survey, I have heard reports of people with GBL habits who quit and had extremely bizarre withdrawal effects – open-eyed 'hallucinations' of elves clambering around for hours fixing non-existent plumbing, that sort of thing. So entity encounters may be a genuine correlate of lactone use, or more specifically a sudden lack of lactone use.

Higher frequency of consumption of specific types of drugs leads to a higher frequency of specific transpersonal or paranormal experiences, like meeting entities on DMT. These results are consistent with the notion that it isn't something particular to the people who use these substances that causes them to report more experiences, but rather that it is the use of the drugs themselves that increases their propensity to have these experiences. I don't think this is news to most people who have taken quantities of psychedelics, say, but strangely this finding has been almost completely unreported anywhere in scientific journals, except in the context of cannabis-induced thought-transmission experiences as symptoms of psychosis. Clearly, lots of people are having such paranormal experiences with psychedelic-type drugs without it causing them psychosis, or else everyone who took these drugs would be in psychiatric care, yet these drug-induced experiences are virtually never discussed within the scientific community. I can only imagine that there are thousands or even millions of people having chemically-inspired paranormal-type experiences and yet it calmly passes without even a whisper within academia.

Source: "A preliminary survey of paranormal experiences with psychoactive drugs" by David P. Luke and Marios Kittenis (2005). Journal of Parapsychology, *69 (2), 305–327*

I myself have only had limited and experimental use of drugs when I was in my late teens, and certainly not Class A drugs. My dependency issues were based on alcohol and during my breakdown prescription pills. Dai and Anne told me they had never taken any form of drugs to their knowledge and were not aware of coming into contact with any substance that would cause such symptoms of hallucinations, psychosis or profound effects on the sensory parts of the brain. Could one conclude that if drugs were the cause that it was being administered nefariously by a yet to be discovered third party?

Gas

Could gas be a cause? There are many forms of gas that have myriad effects from nausea, dizziness, anaemia and even death. Could prolonged exposure to a gas or many gases create the perception of a haunting? Here are a few examples of gas and the effect it can have on people. Could one of these or a mixture be responsible?

Radon is a colourless, odourless substance that's released from the naturally occurring element uranium and can cause serious health problems in those who are exposed to it. Homes with radon problems have been found in Pembrokeshire. Radon exposure is the second leading cause of lung cancer in the United States.

Symptoms can take a long time to develop, so it's very important to have your home tested for radon before developing any serious symptoms. Primary symptoms include severe shortness of breath and coughing (sometimes coughing up blood). Secondary symptoms can include chronic, unexplained fatigue and weight loss, anaemia, dizziness and muscle weakness and unexplained rashes.

Carbon monoxide is odourless, colourless, and impossible to taste or smell. At lower levels of exposure, CO can cause flu-like symptoms, including headaches, dizziness, disorientation, nausea and fatigue. At higher levels, CO exposure can be fatal, which provides another excellent reason to check for its presence when these symptoms are presented.

Sources of carbon monoxide include unvented space heaters, blocked or leaking chimneys, leaking furnaces, gas water heaters, and automobiles in attached garages. An area exposed to CO must be evacuated and ventilated; further exposure can only be prevented by eliminating the source of the gas.

Ozone is a colourless gas that many have heard of in a positive light – the ozone layer that protects us from dangerous solar radiation. Indeed, ozone is beneficial in the atmosphere, but it does not belong in occupied areas, where it poses a danger.

Exposure to ozone can cause numerous respiratory ailments, including throat irritation, coughing, chest pain, and shortness of breath. It will also aggravate the symptoms of those with asthma and other respiratory problems. Longer-term exposure can cause permanent damage, including decreases in lung function and weakened defence against respiratory infection.

Some households and businesses have begun using ozone generators to clean and freshen the indoor air. Ozone generators, which intentionally produce the gas ozone, are often sold as air cleaners despite the dangers of ozone exposure. Additionally, copy machines produce ozone which in a confined space can also cause problems.

The simplest way to avoid ozone exposure is to remove the devices that generate it. Air cleaners that produce ozone – even those that claim to produce it within acceptable ranges – should not be used in the home. Enclosure in a small room, especially, concentrates the gas and may increase the effects.

Sewer gas is typically restricted from entering buildings through plumbing traps that create a water seal at potential points of entry. In addition, plumbing vents allow sewer gases to be exhausted outdoors. Blocked plumbing vents, typically at the roof, also can cause water seals to fail via syphoning of the water.

Exposure to sewer gas also can happen if the gas seeps in via a leaking plumbing drain or vent pipe, or even through cracks in a building's foundation. Sewer gas is typically denser than atmospheric gases and may accumulate in basements, but may eventually mix with surrounding air. Individuals who work in sanitation industries or on farms might be exposed on the job if they clean or maintain municipal sewers, manure storage tanks, or septic tanks.

In most homes, sewer gas may have a slightly unpleasant odour but does not often pose a significant health hazard. Residential sewer pipes primarily contain the gases found in the air such as nitrogen, oxygen and carbon dioxide. Often, methane is the gas of next highest concentration but typically remains at non-toxic levels, especially in properly vented systems. However, if sewer gas has a distinct 'rotten egg' smell, especially in sewage mains, septic tanks, or other sewage treatment facilities, it may be due to hydrogen sulphide content, which can be detected by human olfactory senses in concentrations as low as parts per billion.

Exposure to low levels of this chemical can irritate the eyes, cause a cough or a sore throat, shortness of breath, and fluid accumulation in the lungs. Prolonged low-level exposure may cause fatigue, pneumonia, and loss of appetite, headaches, irritability, poor memory, and dizziness. High concentrations of hydrogen sulphide can produce olfactory fatigue, whereby the scent becomes undetectable. At very high concentrations hydrogen sulphide can cause loss of consciousness and death.

Electromagnetic hypersensitivity (EHS) is a physiological disorder characterised by symptoms directly brought on by exposure to electromagnetic fields. It produces neurological and allergic-type symptoms. Symptoms may include, but are not limited to, headache, eye irritation, dizziness, nausea, skin rash, facial swelling, weakness, fatigue, pain in joints and/or muscles, buzzing/ringing in ears, skin numbness, abdominal pressure and pain, breathing difficulty, and irregular heartbeat. It can also cause what is referred to as a "Fear Cage", which is a high EMF reading in a small room or confined space. It can often cause feelings of uneasiness or paranoia as well as anxiety, which can also create a feeling of being watched, that can lead to the misunderstanding that there is a presence or paranormal being present.

Sources: motorcityghosthunters.com, Wikipedia, independent.co.uk, stayenergysafe.co.uk

I look forward to the day when a full analysis on the house can be conducted. We must be open to the idea that a number of unrelated elements and events could be behind many paranormal phenomena. This, however, does not make the paranormal activity feel any less real to the individuals experiencing them.

Other rationale

There are of course a plethora of other rational explanations that could explain it as well as the notion that this is all an elaborate hoax. What I experienced was extremely real to me. It had a deeply profound effect on my mental and emotional well-being. These occurrences may have been commonplace events misinterpreted as those of a more paranormal origin, and I have always stated that I would accept a valid explanation in the context of all the events perceived. Dai and Anne also consider what they experienced to be real; they did not fabricate it.

I was once asked to investigate a different house on behalf of two parties, acting as a referee, so to speak, in an ongoing family dispute. The house was said to be haunted by the deceased mother of the family. One party wished to sell the house while the other was desperate to keep it in the family so she could remain close to the spirit of the departed matriarch.

The alleged paranormal activity included cold spots and footsteps crossing on the landing and a person said to be crying in the night. This was enough for the person to believe the house was haunted. It took me two hours to distinguish two symptoms. First I discovered missing slates in the roof that had allowed swallows to nest in the attic. The attic hatch was above the landing where the cold spots were said to be. It was easy to deduce the cold spots were no more than a draught cascading from above. Secondly, pipes for the radiators ran the length of the landing, and a few hours after the heating was turned off, the pipes retracted under the floorboards to create the illusion of the sound of someone unseen walking across it. To suggestive minds, these two events could be seen as evidence of paranormal activity. Additionally, on my final night in the house, I finally discovered the cause of the crying.

The house was situated in a rural and isolated part of

Pembrokeshire. The crying seemed to only occur on certain nights. Oddly enough the nights the rubbish was taken out and left on the drive. Clearly, I heard from my room a crying, the crying of a fox. I recorded the sound of the crying and played it back to the lady who was convinced it was her mother's grief at losing the family home. Rational events combined with the desire to believe and the ongoing grief created a very real haunting for the woman. She gave me no thanks for my conclusions.

With suggestion, research has found that believers may have weaker cognitive 'inhibition', compared to sceptics. That's the skill that allows you to quash unwanted thoughts, so perhaps we are all spooked by strange coincidences and patterns from time to time, but sceptics are better at pushing them aside. Paranormal believers also tend to have greater confidence in their decisions, even when they are based on ambiguous information. So once they have latched on to the belief, they might be less likely to let it go.

Even so, most researchers agree that sceptics shouldn't be too critical of people who harbour these beliefs. After all, one study has found that various superstitions can boost your performance in a range of skills. In one trial, subjects bringing their favourite lucky charm into a memory test significantly improved recall, since it seemed to increase their confidence in their own abilities.

And even if you think you are immune, you shouldn't underestimate the power of suggestion. Michael Nees at Lafayette College in Pennsylvania recently asked a group of students to listen to sound recordings from US ghost-hunting shows. Subtly priming the volunteers with the thought that they were involved in a paranormal study increased the number of voices they reported hearing in the fuzzy recordings – despite the fact that they mostly reported being sceptics. It seems that the merest expectation of hearing something spooky can set a mind whirring.

Suggestion is a powerful influence, so much so that in 1958

George Hesketh believed he suffered a personal injury running from a ghost that was said to haunt the location he and his son were working at. Hesketh sued for personal injuries suffered in the course of running away from ghosts at Bush House, a derelict mansion in Pembrokeshire, after he and his son had gone there to lay flooring. Hesketh claimed for a fractured skull after he fell down a staircase. Damages of £1,376 formed an agreed settlement after the judge Lord Justice Salmon acknowledged that the two men had: *"... heard or thought they heard supernatural noises and saw or thought they saw a ghost."*

One has to ask oneself if Hesketh would have suffered an injury if the mansion did not have the anecdote of a ghost attached to it.

Claire Elliot is researching paranormal belief and Electronic Voice Phenomena (*EVP*) for her MSc at Manchester Metropolitan University and a member of the British Psychological Society, Society for Psychical Research and founding member of the MMU Parapsychology Society, and has this to evaluate on the subject as presented on her blog, *The Claire Witch Files*.

There are many cognitive mechanisms and biases (short cuts) we use to process the available information to understand the world in a 'good-enough-fit' model. Our ancestors wouldn't have lasted very long if they'd contemplated everything before reacting. Here's a small selection of the salient ones in relation to paranormal phenomena:

Confirmation Bias Tendency to favour and recall information that confirms our existing beliefs and not searching for enough alternative evidence. I think this is why I always feel 'dirty' reading the *Daily Mail*.

Hindsight Bias *"I knew it all along!"* The sense that an event was predictable despite having no basis for predicting it that memory becomes reconstructed, i.e. forgets contrary evidence. We tend to remember the hits, not the misses.

Pareidolia Seeing something significant (*i.e. a pattern*) in random information. This can be both visual and auditory. Common examples include Faces in Places and Electronic Voice Phenomena (*EVP*).

Anthropomorphism The attribution of human traits, emotions, intentions to non-human objects and entities, e.g. weather, animals. Animals, of course, have emotions and intentions but dressing them up, giving them birthday parties and marriage ceremonies says more about us than them.

Agency Detection Bias Tendency to falsely believe phenomena are explainable in terms of an active conscious agent, closely linked to anthropomorphism.

Type 1 Error A false positive (*incorrect rejection of the null hypothesis*). It's safer in evolutionary terms to assume a perceived threat is real than false (*Type 2 error, false negative/incorrect acceptance of the null hypothesis*).

False Memory Recall of memories that did not occur. Most of us have experienced this in some small way but it has had big implications for criminal cases.

So it's worth being critical of our own perceptions and the testimony of others. How many times have we heard people say *I know what I saw!* Can we fully know what we have seen? Paranormal experiences are usually in ambiguous conditions, i.e. night time, peripheral vision, fleeting etc. I often qualify my evidence with, *"This may be a false memory or a dream but..."*

This may be extreme but it appears we can't always trust our own perception.

Sources: bbc.com, culteducation.com, Daily Express *28th March 1958,* Fortean Times *FT332, "Ghost Brain: Why we THINK we see things" by Claire Elliot/clairewitchfiles.blogspot.co.uk*

Supernatural

Let us explore the ying to the rational's yang and identify possible otherworldly explanations for the events of the house.

Before sceptics and rationalists dismiss this section of thought I would like to remind you of historical academics such as Galileo Galilei who was persecuted for contradicting the beliefs and understanding the people of his era held. He would, of course, go on to become the father of modern science.

Perhaps we should quickly reflect on the work of Marcelino Sanz de Sautuola, an amateur archaeologist who discovered the Altamira cave in 1875, now famous for its unique collection of prehistoric art, and concluded that man had been around for longer than we had first believed. However, the scientific community was reluctant to accept the presumed antiquity of the paintings or the notion we were far older as a race. It was not until 1902, when several other findings of prehistoric paintings had served to render the hypothesis of the extreme antiquity of the Altamira paintings less shocking (and forgery less likely), that the scientific society retracted their opposition to the Spaniard. That year, the towering French archaeologist Émile Cartailhac, who had been one of the leading critics, emphatically admitted his mistake in the famous article, "Mea culpa d'un sceptique", published in the journal *L'Anthropologie*.

Why is this relevant to a book on the paranormal? Simply because we cannot as a race be so arrogant to think we know everything there is to know about everything when our history shows us examples of erroneous and destructive thinking and how we can inhibit progress by not exploring every possibility. I cannot comprehend how some people think today that in a decade or a century or millennia our understanding of how we interpret the world, the universe and everything we know will still be valid. So, with an open mind, let's look at these preternatural phenomena.

Source: britannica.com, Escritos y documentos – *1976 by M. Sanz De Sautuola*

Ghosts, Spirits and Hauntings

The case at the house in Haverfordwest has exhibited many of the classic symptoms of a haunting. If we remove the ideas of a being not created from the fabric of our universe being involved then we do have typical paranormal activity. The cause of events would be a ghost or spirit.

A ghost is said to be the soul or spirit of a dead person or animal that can appear to the living. Descriptions of ghosts vary widely from an invisible presence to translucent or barely visible wispy shapes, to realistic, lifelike visions. People in this field of the study of the paranormal say that Ghosts and Spirits are two very different entities. However, a ghost has more negative connotations attached whereas spirits tend to be more benevolent, but both are essentially the same as they live in the same realm and have the same kind of energy.

Temperature receding to unpleasant lows, smells, voices, electrical interference and of course the now in vogue paranormal visitor, shadow people, are common in many reported hauntings across the UK. Traditional hauntings are upgrading in their capacity to dumbfound and terrorize but the house in Haverfordwest does have the principal symptoms that can be likened to other hauntings.

The Haverfordwest House would be classified as an intelligent haunting. An intelligent haunting is described as a haunting in which the spirit or ghost demonstrates an intelligence level at which the entity seems to be aware of its surroundings and the present-day situation. These ghosts have been said to actually communicate or interact with the living. Intelligent hauntings often involve objects being moved and other physical activity such as the spirits making sounds, noises, writing on walls, mirrors, slamming doors, and other physical traits such as footsteps appearing from nowhere. There have been reports of intelligent hauntings where the entities will move things around or even hide objects from their living counterparts.

Distinct smells and/or odours are also commonly reported with intelligent hauntings.

If we conclude it is a haunting, then who is responsible for the haunting? The prime suspects would have to be the family that lived there around 1890 to 1910, based on the information given, although from dreams and visions, which sadly we cannot build an accurate case study from. No records can be found to cement the identity of these people. Did they even exist?

There are of course other residents of the home including a man that died of a terminal illness and maybe it was his face that was claimed to be seen in the headboard. Were there multiple spirits haunting that house, including animal spirits? Was the house haunted?

Sources: Encyclopaedia of the Paranormal *by Gordon Stein;* An Introduction to Parapsychology, *5th ed. by Harvey J. Irwin, Caroline A. Watt;* Oxford Dictionary of English *edited by Angus Stevenson*

Time concurrence

Were the horrid people that lived in the house a century before responsible for the events there without actually being ghosts at all? Anne's visit into their time seems to indicate that both Anne and the family could be perceived to one another with direct communication and influence on the environment they travelled to. In the film *The Others* directed by Alejandro Amenábar and starring Nicole Kidman, it was suggested two distinct times were crossing over each other so people from either one were affecting the other, haunting each other so to speak. Could this be a possible explanation for the events in Haverfordwest?

The children in the house and the old woman were both aware of Anne's presence in their time. Anne also claimed that she could interact to some degree with her surroundings, making choices and performing actions in that world. Even though it was described as a dream state, it is a worthwhile theory to contemplate.

What conditions would be needed for events where two times could cross over? Could this other famous paranormal character from Haverfordwest solidify the theory? One of the more popular Pembrokeshire hauntings has to be the hooded monk regularly seen walking silently and submerged into the pavement at Union Hill. He makes his way down the hill that many locals have walked or driven. From the waist down he is invisible as he travels a long-buried and forgotten footpath. This shadowy spectre has been seen many times with the first known report made in 1729 of a cowled and dark apparition making its way to the old Augustinian priory.

Mr Rob Richards of Haverfordwest reminisced about a sighting, in the 1950s, at the end of Quay Street where a hooded figure was said to disappear into a gate at the bottom of Union Hill, while more recent reports have seen a hooded figure making its way up Tower Hill at the top of Haverfordwest, and another seeing a monk-like figure traversing the Rifleman's Field near Winch Lane.

Are people witnessing the monk walk the path in his time? Is it conceivable that as we see the monk he is just as startled to see us and quickly makes his way back to the priory with his heart banging in his chest after witnessing such a strange and out of place character staring back at him?

How many hauntings describe the startling activity of a ghost walking through a wall only to discover at a later date that a door had once existed in that space decades or centuries before. Imagine, if you will, yourself sat on your sofa watching the TV when a shadowy shape walks pasts and vanishes into the wall. You shout in fear and amazement, maybe leaping to your feet. Now again, imagine the shadow is not a paranormal being at all but just an ordinary person going about their business in their time; it's the same place, same location, just a different time, and as this person walks through the room they hear a muffled talking, feel a presence, hear shouting and someone moving behind them. How petrified would that person be?

Living people not so much haunting but interacting with the same space but different times. You could, in essence, be interacting with someone in the past, the future and even yourself!

Could this theory explain all the events that happened at the house? If you reread the testimonies with this theory in mind I believe that some sense could be made of the activity that occurred there.

Sources: theparanormalchronicles.com, IMDB.com

Demonic

Paranormal aficionados are no doubt familiar with the subject of demons and demonic activity through mainstream media. Movies such as the 1973 movie *The Exorcist* directed by William Friedkin or the 1981 offering *The Evil Dead* directed by Sam Raimi have popularised the idea of demonic entities, activity and possession.

A demon is a supernatural and often malevolent being prevalent in religion, occultism, literature, fiction, mythology and folklore, and is considered an unclean spirit, a fallen angel, or a spirit of unknown type. Many hold the belief that demonic entities are from Hell. Hell is a place or state of torment and punishment in the afterlife and has been written into our mythological and religious doctrines as another dimension or a place under the Earth's surface, and often includes entrances to Hell from the land of the living. This is said to be the Domain of the Devil.

The Bible provides abundant evidence of the existence of demons. Satan's evil angels are known in Scripture as demons. We know from certain Scriptures that Satan fell from Heaven and other angelic beings (demons) shared in Satan's fall and became evil (Ezekiel 28:18; Matthew 25:41; Revelation 12:4).

The word for demons in the Greek language is daimon and

is found more than 75 times in the *Greek New Testament*. In each case, it is translated into the word devil in the *King James Version*. In Jesus Christ's teachings and ministry, He often confronted demons and their activities, i.e. demonic possession of individuals (Matthew 12:22–29, 15:22–28, 25:41; Mark 5:1–16). Christ demonstrated His power over demons and, furthermore, He gave His disciples power to cast out demons (Matthew 10:1). One theory that is most likely is that demons are fallen angels who rebelled against God in Heaven and were cast out of the presence of God. As such, what things are true about the nature of good angels are also true of demons.

Another contemporary idea relating to the origins of demons claims they are the spirits of the evil dead. This is the underlying assumption of much of the popular occult literature while others have suggested that demons are the result of the union of angels and women as described:

> *The Nephilim (giants) were on the earth in those days, and also afterwards when the sons of God came into the daughters of man and they bore children to them. These were the mighty men who were of old, the men of renown.*
> *– Genesis 6:4*

Demons attack in a number of ways. Examples provided in the Bible include physical illness, mental impairment, the spread of false doctrine, spiritual warfare and possession.

Could the house in Haverfordwest be a portal that allows the creatures of Hell to torment the living, causing mental suffering, anguish and a decay of the soul? Demonologists have theorised that some forms of mental diseases can also be attributed to demons. In at least two cases of demon possession treated by Jesus during His ministry, the demons had so affected the minds of the victims to cause abnormal behaviour.

Had a demonic entity attached itself to the mysterious family that had lived there and tempted them to engage in immoral practices? Is there a demon residing there hungry for new souls? Is it there to tarnish everything it influences? Has it used its powers to confound, terrorize and disintegrate the ordinary lives of people?

Rose had said it was a place beyond Hell that she had seen during her visit; but Anne pondered, what if what she was seeing was a version of Hell? With a demon's ability to trick and entice surely it could shroud itself in a veil of the obscure and the sadistic to chip away at the foundations of self. Despite at least two alleged spiritual or mediumistic people unsuccessfully attempting to cleanse the house, I have wondered what would have happened if an exorcism should have been or could be conducted at the residence.

Jennifer Malek, broadcaster and resident Demonologist for the Northern Wisconsin Paranormal Society, has dealt with demons personally and has written about her experiences, which she believes will help those understand and protect themselves from demonic activity. This is an extract from her *How to safeguard and protect yourself from the demonic*:

I would like to explain the levels in which they operate, from temptation to possession, and the ultimate goal of the demonic, which is death.

But first I need to explain about a process called scout and roam. This is where the high-level demons (*seven princes of Hell*) will send in their *minions*. They are simply sent to check out a home and the family who resides there.

After they gather the information needed, they then report back to the demon that they are serving, and fill this demon in on what they saw and heard while they were present. They may find for instance that someone in the home drinks, while the other takes drugs. They look for any kind of illnesses the residents may have, such as any abuse in the home, and if so, who causes it. These are some of the things done during a scout and roam.

The first stage is called temptation, which takes place when things like Ouija and occult practices are carried out in the home. Knowingly or unknowingly, both can and do open doorways for them to enter in. Things that have the look and feel of dark energy to them can get their attention. [Is] there excessive drug and alcohol use in the home? Does anyone watch horror movies or even porn? All of these things factor in the temptation stage as well as religious beliefs or lack thereof, or none whatsoever.

The second stage is an infestation, which can happen after the scout and roam process takes place. The higher-level demon enters the home and finds a place to work from inside the home.

This is when the feeling and energy in the home changes from normal, calm, and peaceful, to very heavy, negative, and oppressive. This is followed by the feeling of constantly being watched in every area of the home, followed by shadows, cold spots, objects that go missing or are moved. Smells such as sulphur, garbage, sewage, decay, and in some cases fecal matter! The smells are there for long or short periods of time. Knocks and bangs in threes occur.

The third stage is oppression, which occurs when the demon will work on breaking down each family member one at a time until they are fighting with each other. They can and do cause financial problems, vehicle problems, things may start to break down in the home, and they cause breakups and divorces.

The fourth stage is obsession, which occurs when the demon has singled out one person in the home and will use their fears to break that person down. They will cause major depression, and get physical with them, such as biting, scratching, and in some cases get sexual. They will do whatever they can to get to the next stage which is possession.

Possession takes place after obsession, in which the demon has gotten inside of the oppressed person. Without any help, this will ultimately lead to their end goal... and that is death.

Here are ways you can safeguard and protect yourself and loved ones from all of the above. First, build up your spiritual armor with yourself and God. Get rid of anything in the home that has a negative look and feel to it. A baptism would be a very good thing to have done if no one in the home has had one, but has thought about it.

Holy water and blessed oil, as well as salt, can be obtained from a church. Anoint the doorways and windows with it, as well as each other. Prayer is important here! Daily and nightly prayers, such as the prayer to St. Michael, or the St. Benedict prayer. If you are Catholic, recite the rosary. Teach your kids to do this as well. Nightlights in the children's rooms work because demons do not like the light!

Holy relics and medals also work. Use crucifixes, not just crosses, as crucifixes have the image of Jesus on them and the demonic are repelled by this. Crosses without Him are useless and will not work.

St. Michaels medals, St. Benedicts medals, and the Miraculous Medal (with Mary on it) should be worn on each household member and kept on them at all times.

Most importantly is to show no fear, as to not give them any power over you in any way! Have your house blessed once a week for every month, and say your own prayers.

Do not talk to them or communicate with them in any way, shape or form. After a while, they will get tired and find someone else to bug.

These methods will help you to be aware, alert and safe.

Exorcism is the religious or spiritual practice of purportedly evicting demons or other spiritual entities from a person or an area they are believed to have possessed. Depending on the spiritual beliefs of the exorcist, this may be done by causing the entity to swear an oath, performing an elaborate ritual, or simply by commanding it to depart in the name of a higher power. The practice is ancient and part of the belief system of many cultures and religions.

Requested and performed exorcisms had begun to decline in the United States by the 18th century and occurred rarely until the latter half of the 20th century when the public saw a sharp rise due to the media attention exorcisms were getting. There was a 50% increase in the number of exorcisms performed between the early 1960s and the mid-1970s.

Should access to the house be agreeable, and once a study has been conducted, one would imagine that an exorcism may very well be a key to extinguishing the evil that resides there for good. However, based on personal experience it could not only agitate the force that preys there but worse still increase its power to unimaginable levels.

Sources: King James Bible, Greek New Testament, *"How to safeguard and protect yourself from the demonic" by Jennifer Malek,* The Dictionary of Demons *by Michelle Belanger,* Demons in the Bible: A Scriptural Look at the Subject of Demons *by Sonny Shanks, Wikipedia, IMDB.com*

Alien intrusion

This may be a surprising entry into the collection of suspects but one I have considered at great length. I have been conducting a study, parallel to the one you have before you, into a young lady's claim that she has been the focus of alien abduction, interaction and/or more commonly known as a Close Encounter of the Fourth Kind which defines a UFO event in which a human is abducted by a UFO or its occupants.

The reason I found it so intriguing was how the aliens chose to communicate through surreal imagery, dreams and visions, and how they would be seen passing through her home as shadowy entities. Could this be what was happening at that home in Haverfordwest?

Why would alien beings from another world be so interested in a house in Haverfordwest and could such things exist?

Extraterrestrial life, also called alien life, is life that does not originate from Earth. These hypothetical life forms may range from simple single-celled organisms to beings with civilisations far more advanced than humanity. Although many scientists expect extraterrestrial life to exist in some form, there is no publicly disclosed evidence for its existence to date.

Many other planets throughout the universe probably hosted intelligent life long before Earth did. The probability of a civilisation developing on a potentially habitable alien planet would have to be less than one in 10 billion trillion – or one part in 10 to the 22nd power – for humanity to be the first technologically advanced species the cosmos has ever known, according to a study. Could it be we are not alone in the universe?

The UFO and alien phenomena have been a relatively new occurrence in the scheme of all things supernatural, unless of course the demons and the fairies, mythical gods and creatures, and the angels were simply misidentified alien visitors studying or manipulating our race of people.

Since 1945, though, sightings have been recorded in ancient texts and cave paintings; there has been a surge in UFO sightings which has been attributed to the military, space programs, weather effects, birds, time travellers and Nazis hiding in the Antarctic among many but disclosure from the governments of the world have been (purposefully) lackadaisical.

What would a sophisticated race of beings want with us? What would be their motives? Had the people in Haverfordwest, including myself, been part of an alien infringement?

I hope that continued work into my new project into the claims of alien abduction and the abstruse methods of visual communication and stimulation may couple the account to the one of the house. I look forward to sharing my findings with you at a later date. Until that time this theory has no supporting evidence.

Sources: project1947.com, space.com, Wikipedia, UFO Sightings Desk Reference *by Cheryl Costa*

Dimensional entity

I have purposefully left this hypothesis to the end. There are of course many other ideas that we could be presented with, but this is the one I have had to give much consideration to. There is very little to reference it by. There is scarce information on similar occurrences out there to correlate to, and most of this is conjecture. So why is it included?

Rose believed after her decades of personal experience fighting off all manner of entities, helping spirits pass and supporting families enduring living nightmares that what she was dealing with was not anything she had encountered before. She told Dai it frightened her and her description of it was based on her mind trying to make sense of something unimaginable.

Now based on the ideas you have read, it could have merely been a selection of rational elements and conditions that encouraged the perception of a prolonged paranormal event; or with contraposition thinking, one could argue it was a demonic entity, terrible and cruel, manipulating the events at the house.

So if a dimensional entity were to exist then where does this thing come from? The universe we live in may not be the only one out there. In fact, our universe could be just one of an infinite number of universes making up a *multiverse*. Though the concept may stretch credulity, there's good physics behind it. And there's not just one way to get to a *multiverse*. Numerous physics theories independently point to such a conclusion. In fact, some experts think the existence of hidden universes is more likely than not.

Another idea that arises from string theory is the notion of *braneworlds*, parallel universes that hover just out of reach of our own, proposed by Princeton University's Paul Steinhardt and

Neil Turok of the Perimeter Institute for Theoretical Physics in Ontario, Canada. The idea comes from the possibility of many more dimensions to our world than the three of space and one of time that we know. In addition to our own three-dimensional *brane* of space, other three-dimensional branes may float in a higher-dimensional space.

If this is to be true then how long has man known about this? Is this is a relatively new theory? Maybe not. Many ancient cultures speak of portals to other worlds and gateways to star systems where their creators reside. Conventional wisdom tells us these tales are merely myths and legends.

The Abu Sir Pyramids, site of Abu Ghurab, has claimed to be one of the oldest sites on the planet. Within Abu Ghurab lies an ancient platform made of alabaster (*Egyptian crystal*) and is said to be in tune with the vibration of Earth. It can also open the senses for a person to communicate and be one with higher, sacred energies of the universe. Interestingly, legends of communication and a way of travel between other worlds and ours almost mirror the legends of the Cherokee Native Americans. The Cherokee tell of thought beings, which are formless and could travel on a wave of sound. There are so many ancient legends and myths from all corners of the world, separated by seas and lands, all focusing on travel to other dimensions and other parts of the universe.

The ancient Egyptians' version of Hell was one of another worldly entity, a deity that would torture in every imaginable way and destroyed wrongdoers and consigned them to non-existence. They were deprived of their sense organs, were required to walk on their heads and eat their own excrement. They were phased from existence.

Have the evils of old been dimensional beings that have seeped through dimensional rifts into the fabric of our world to absorb and harvest our souls, to leech off us and phase us out of existence? Can we truly fathom the nature and thought process of something that does not reside in anything we can currently comprehend?

How long have they been here and what is their purpose? How many of these entities reside here? Is their intent to harm unintentional and by their mere presence, manipulating their surroundings, creating a nightmare of perception? How many homes across the world have something unimaginable seeping through unseen tears in the dimensional divides? Rose said the entity at the home in Haverfordwest was connected to a greater, larger entity; it was part of a hub. Where did this hub stem to? Is our world on the prelude to invasion… or much worse? Could in time our world be phased out and absorbed by something far greater than anything we can comprehend. We can't fight what we can't understand.

God did not create it, God had no domain over it and the Devil feared it.

Sources: The Truth Revealed – Volume 6 by Derek Barclay, landofpyramids.org, bibliotecapleyades.net, bbc.co.uk, space.com, societyofmodernastronomy.wordpress.com

Thank you to Dave Dominguez, Susan Taylor, GV Thomas, Kevin and Jennifer Malek, Claire Elliot, Kat Hobson, Christina George, Kathryn Ashworth, Nikki Davies, Elaine Sugden Kelly, Jason Bland, Bryan Alvarez, Keith Anthony Blanchard, Dale Boswell, Christina McKee Horrocks, Tim Wiseberg, Tubbsy R. Jones, S. Dukes, Matt Giles, Claire Lyford, Ross Raposso, Kevin Moore, Kath Williams, James Vaughn Thomas, Keryn Williams and DJ Jones for your discussion, contributions and support throughout this project.

An Interview with GL Davies

May 2015

The Paranormal Chronicles' very own DJ Jones sits down with founder of The Paranormal Chronicles, paranormal investigator GL Davies, author of the Kindle number 1 bestselling novel, *A most haunted house*, to find out just what makes him so compelled to delve deep into the unknown.

First of all, we would like to congratulate you on your success of *A most haunted house*. It has topped the charts in two Kindle sections and even outsold the Dalai Lama's book. Did you ever expect your novel to be so widely appreciated?

GL Davies: *(Laughing)* I don't think I have outsold the Dalai Lama's book, but for one day I sold a few more copies and was one position above him. I have had a keen passion for the paranormal since I was a child and have had a deep interest, and the events of the house had to be told. I never expected it to sell over 20,000 copies in little over a year, and I certainly did not expect it to become a number 1 bestseller. People from all over the world are reading about Haverfordwest!!

I am humbled and grateful to everyone that took the time to read it, supported it, and I have enjoyed all the feedback, interest and correspondence because of it. So many people have been so kind. People I live by and worked with got behind it from day one and I was amazed. I can't thank them enough. It's been a very interesting part of my life.

***A most haunted house* has been seen as controversial for many reasons by many people. Would you care to explain why this is?**

GL Davies: Whenever you deal with any topic within the

paranormal, you are always going to deal with some controversy. For a paranormal world to exist then that can affect society on so many levels whether it is religion, science, medicine, biology, zoology, philosophy or sociological. Each individual on this planet has their own belief system so to tell one person that a ghost can interact on a destructive scale and affect people's lives may be insulting, certainly challenging to what they know; where another person can happily believe and be convinced with no shred of evidence as that is what they wish to choose to be the case.

I have had emails from people asking me for help and guidance, an opinion and so on in regards to their own experiences, and I have had some say I am encouraging the belief of dark practices and I am encouraging people to foolishly dabble in something diabolical. Sceptics have asked how I could write about such things when science has not proven such things exist. I think also because the book centres on a relationship break-up which is described in a very raw and detailed manner that some people find that unsettling. It has upset quite a few people that something so terrible could do so much damage.

What did you reply to the sceptics?

GL Davies: I replied that as far as we know science has not been able – to my knowledge – to create such phenomena in lab conditions. However, not so long ago in human history we believed the world to be flat, that the sun rotated around the Earth. We used to burn those in tune with nature, those that participated in holistic practices as witches as it did not fit in with the popular religious beliefs of the time. That is an awful tragic part of our legacy. I am not an 'open as a barn door' believer, but there is room for everyone to just think, "What if?"

Society, in my opinion, needs to challenge what we believe we know and question and push for more solid answers. We are a very spiritual race when you look at it. We have a religious, theological and philosophical awareness. I believe there may be a reason for that other than a nagging fear of death, the journey into the unknown. Over millennia I believe that we have inherited a bond with the universe and the universe has so many unknown elements that we cannot fathom. Compared to what our universe has, our knowledge is merely a grain of sand on a beach. It shouldn't be a frightening prospect but an exciting and marvellous one.

In *A most haunted house,* the haunting seems to focus on a couple and their vulnerability. What motive can you speculate the entity had?

GL Davies: Whatever was in that house was creating a very negative emotional response from the people there. It was almost as if it was trying to see how hard it could push them to break point, and then just as they were about to break it would pull back, enough to create a sense of hope, of rest, and then start up again with a more intensified relentlessness. With the people, I saw anger, confusion, sadness and fear among other things.

Over the 25-plus years I have investigated there are instances where I have been able to dissect the truth from the fiction. Some people like to feel that something special is happening to them as they feel life does not offer them enough. That perhaps life is mundane or that they are insignificant and need to feel chosen or victimized. When you read the book you get a sense from that, something awful and uncontrollable was occurring and not in an outlandish and exaggerated way but a slow and gradual build-up. It's not all about blood pouring out of the walls and heads spinning around spewing pea soup.

You have spoken out about some paranormal investigators not actually being very good investigators.

GL Davies: There are some fantastic investigators but I have spoken out in general that some paranormal investigators simply feel that wandering around with cameras at night shouting, "Show yourself!" is tantamount to a thorough investigation. That is fine but I believe the real investigation is the human element; deciphering what really happened. Body language, the delivery of the words, the expression and detail given in witness testimonials hold the real clues to what is happening.

Investigators need to discover the motives and origins of the event first. Get the story, cross-examine the people involved if possible with thorough interview techniques, then do your research and then conduct the field study. That's my opinion. *(Laughing)* I think this is based on some experiences I have had with some terrible investigators.

Could you give an example?

GL Davies: There was this one group that toured around and would charge for an evening in an alleged and historic haunted location. I actually went to two of them as, for whatever my opinion, [it] was very good at securing some pretty spectacular locations. One night I caught one throwing a chair and then saying the chair was thrown at him; another man was throwing stones at people in a séance saying they were spirits. I actually filmed him doing it on a night vision camera, and when I presented it to him he said he must have been processed by a mischievous witch. There were many, many examples.

Have you ever been afraid of an investigation?

GL Davies: Definitely and that's part of the thrill, part of why I do it. The adrenaline starts to pump but you have to be careful that you don't let your irrationality overwhelm you. Evidence has to be gathered, and the mindset no matter what you are witnessing has to be of what is actually happening here. One time in Pembroke Castle I think I was the most confused and terrified. I wrote an article about it called the "Stinking men of Pembroke Dock".

Not only has *A most haunted house* been a commercial success but critically you have had some very good reviews. How does that feel?

GL Davies: I wrote the novel while I was waiting at train stations. I liked the idea of having a found footage element that you have in so many films but in a paranormal account, so chose to document it as an interview rather than a story-based narrative. I thought it might be a risk but then I genuinely only thought a handful of people would read it. I have received some very positive reviews. Even the constructive ones I appreciate as it's the only way I can learn and grow as a writer.

I am working on a new project and if I can eliminate some of the mistakes and errors then hopefully people can enjoy them more. I am dyslexic and thrilled by the response of *A most haunted house*. Nearly four and a half stars out of five from 107 reviews is very humbling. I never thought it would connect to readers in the way it has, and so many people email me with great stories of their own and with theories on what happened at the house in Haverfordwest. It is a remarkable and thrilling experience. I am so blessed, I cannot thank people enough. Everyone that has read my work has had such a profound effect on my life. Thank you so much.

What is your favourite ghost novel of all time?

GL Davies: It has to be *Green Tea* by J. Sheridan Le Fanu. If people reading this have not read it then please do so. Plus any *Family Guy* fans that like the evil monkey will love it. It's about a vicar in Victorian England that drinks too much green tea and is haunted by an evil monkey. It's a great story that really shows how the world was changing at the time, and the book is about Eastern religion, Darwinism and the church all trying to coinhabit a changing world, great story. Plus anything by MR James.

Have you a degree module in hauntings in 19th century literature?

GL Davies: I do, amazing course, would recommend it to anyone.

As well as having written *A most haunted house,* founding The Paranormal Chronicles, being a paranormal investigator, you won ITV1's *Natural Born Sellers* in 2008, appeared on the Harry Hill TV show, *TV Burp* (Season 8, Episode 1), were a cobbler and watch repairer, and you studied to be a barber, and currently work in advertising. You seem to have achieved quite a lot by 39. What motivates you?

GL Davies: *(Laughing)* I want to have an eclectic mix of people at my funeral, I want to have the most interesting funeral ever!

GL Davies can be contacted at paranormalchronicles@aol.com and his articles can be read at www.theparanormalchronicles.com.

6th Books

ALL THINGS PARANORMAL

Investigations, explanations and deliberations on the paranormal, supernatural, explainable or unexplainable. 6th Books seeks to give answers while nourishing the soul: whether making use of the scientific model or anecdotal and fun, but always beautifully written.

Titles cover everything within parapsychology: how to, lifestyles, alternative medicine, beliefs, myths and theories.

If you have enjoyed this book, why not tell other readers by posting a review on your preferred book site? Recent bestsellers from 6th Books are:

The Afterlife Unveiled

What the Dead Are Telling us About Their World!

Stafford Betty

What happens after we die? Spirits speaking through mediums know, and they want us to know. This book unveils their world…

Paperback: 978-1-84694-496-3 ebook: 978-1-84694-926-5

Spirit Release

Sue Allen

A guide to psychic attack, curses, witchcraft, spirit attachment, possession, soul retrieval, haunting, deliverance, exorcism and more, as taught at the College of Psychic Studies.

Paperback: 978-1-84694-033-0 ebook: 978-1-84694-651-6

I'm Still With You

True Stories of Healing Grief Through Spirit Communication

Carole J. Obley

A series of after-death spirit communications which uplift, comfort and heal, and show how love helps us grieve.

Paperback: 978-1-84694-107-8 ebook: 978-1-84694-639-4

Less Incomplete

A Guide to Experiencing the Human Condition Beyond the Physical Body

Sandie Gustus

Based on 40 years of scientific research, this book is a dynamic guide to understanding life beyond the physical body.

Paperback: 978-1-84694-351-5 ebook: 978-1-84694-892-3

Advanced Psychic Development

Becky Walsh

Learn how to practise as a professional, contemporary spiritual medium.

Paperback: 978-1-84694-062-0 ebook: 978-1-78099-941-8

Astral Projection Made Easy

Overcoming the Fear of Death

Stephanie June Sorrell

From the popular Made Easy series, *Astral Projection Made Easy* helps to eliminate the fear of death, through discussion of life beyond the physical body.

Paperback: 978-1-84694-611-0 ebook: 978-1-78099-225-9

The Miracle Workers Handbook
Seven Levels of Power and Manifestation of the Virgin Mary
Sherrie Dillard
Learn how to invoke the Virgin Mary's presence, communicate with her, receive her grace and miracles and become a miracle worker.
Paperback: 978-1-84694-920-3 ebook: 978-1-84694-921-0

An Angels' Guide to Working with the Power of Light
Laura Newbury
Discovering her ability to communicate with angels, Laura Newbury records her inspirational messages of guidance and answers to universal questions.
Paperback: 978-1-84694-908-1 ebook: 978-1-84694-909-8

Does It Rain in Other Dimensions?
A True Story of Alien Encounters
Mike Oram
We have neighbors in the universe. This book describes one man's experience of communicating with other-dimensional and extra-terrestrial beings over a 50-year period.
Paperback: 978-1-84694-054-5

Readers of ebooks can buy or view any of these bestsellers by clicking on the live link in the title. Most titles are published in paperback and as an ebook. Paperbacks are available in traditional bookshops. Both print and ebook formats are available online.
Find more titles and sign up to our readers' newsletter at http://www.johnhuntpublishing.com/mind-body-spirit.
Follow us on Facebook at https://www.facebook.com/OBooks and Twitter at https://twitter.com/obooks.